School-Based Drug Prevention

What Kind of Drug Use Does It Prevent?

Jonathan P. Caulkins
Rosalie Liccardo Pacula
Susan Paddock
James Chiesa

Prepared for the
Robert Wood Johnson Foundation

Drug Policy Research Center

RAND

The research described in this report was supported by The Robert Wood Johnson Foundation's Substance Abuse Policy Research Program. Additional support was provided by RAND's Drug Policy Research Center with funding from the Ford Foundation.

Library of Congress Cataloging-in-Publication Data

School-based drug prevention : what kind of drug use does it prevent? / Jonathan P.
Caulkins ... [et al.].
     p. cm.
     "MR-1459."
     Includes bibliographical references.
     ISBN 0-8330-3082-5
     1. Students—Drug use—United States. 2. Youth—Drug use—United States. 3.
Drug abuse—United States—Prevention. I. Caulkins, Jonathan P. (Jonathan Paul),
1965– II. Rand Corporation.

HV5824.Y68 S337 2002
362.29'17'0973—dc21

                                                                              2002068

RAND is a nonprofit institution that helps improve policy and decisionmaking through research and analysis. RAND® is a registered trademark. RAND's publications do not necessarily reflect the opinions or policies of its research sponsors.

Published 2002 by RAND
1700 Main Street, P.O. Box 2138, Santa Monica, CA 90407-2138
1200 South Hayes Street, Arlington, VA 22202-5050
201 North Craig Street, Suite 202, Pittsburgh, PA 15213-1516
RAND URL: http://www.rand.org/
To order RAND documents or to obtain additional information,
contact Distribution Services: Telephone: (310) 451-7002;
Fax: (310) 451-6915; Email: order@rand.org

Prevention is one of three principal approaches to controlling the use of illicit drugs in the United States. While the cost-effectiveness of the other two approaches—enforcement and treatment—had been the subject of analyses in the mid-1990s, prevention had not been addressed. That gap was filled in 1999 with the publication of *An Ounce of Prevention, a Pound of Uncertainty* (MR-923-RWJ) by RAND's Drug Policy Research Center. That study, funded by the Robert Wood Johnson Foundation, assessed just how cost-effective prevention was at controlling cocaine use both in absolute terms and relative to other types of drug control interventions. As the title of that report suggests, considerable uncertainty attends the cost-effectiveness estimates, but a bottom-line finding was that school-based drug prevention can be competitive with other programs that currently receive more attention and more resources as a means of reducing cocaine use.

Unlike drug enforcement, however, school-based prevention also generates benefits by reducing the use of licit substances, specifically alcohol and tobacco, as well as illicit ones. The research described in this book, also funded by the Robert Wood Johnson Foundation, updates and extends the earlier work to cover prevention's effects on a full range of substances. In particular, the study team examines which substances are principally responsible for prevention's benefits when the use of those substances is reduced; that is, given that prevention programs affect the use of different substances differently, and that some substances are more costly to society than others, we estimate how a dollar's investment in prevention may generate greater or lesser reductions in social cost from reductions in the use of one substance versus another. This book should be of interest to policymakers and researchers who are interested in drug prevention and drug policy more generally.

This book is the latest in a series from RAND's Drug Policy Research Center addressing costs and benefits of different approaches to drug use prevention. The others are:

- Jonathan P. Caulkins, C. Peter Rydell, Susan S. Everingham, James Chiesa, and Shawn Bushway, *An Ounce of Prevention, a Pound of Uncertainty: The Cost-Effectiveness of School-Based Drug Prevention Programs,* MR-923-RWJ, 1999.

- Jonathan P. Caulkins, C. Peter Rydell, William L. Schwabe, and James Chiesa, *Mandatory Minimum Drug Sentences: Throwing Away the Key or the Taxpayers' Money?* MR-827-DPRC, 1997.

- Jonathan P. Caulkins, Nora Fitzgerald, Karyn Model, and H. Lamar Willis, *Youth Drug Prevention Through Community Outreach: The Military's Pilot Programs,* MR-536-OSD, 1994.

- Susan S. Everingham and C. Peter Rydell, *Modeling the Demand for Cocaine,* MR-332-ONDCP/A/DPRC, 1994.

- C. Peter Rydell and Susan S. Everingham, *Controlling Cocaine: Supply Versus Demand Programs,* MR-331-ONDCP/A/DPRC, 1994.

The Drug Policy Research Center examines drug use trends and assesses drug control strategies for various sponsors. The center, coadministered by RAND Public Safety and Justice and RAND Health, draws on core support from The Ford Foundation to sustain drug-research-related databases and to ensure broad dissemination of research results.

CONTENTS

FIGURES

SUMMARY

Drug use prevention programs are now commonplace in the nation's schools. Their aim is to prevent, or at least delay or diminish, children's use of a variety of substances, including illicit drugs such as marijuana and cocaine and licit substances such as alcohol and tobacco. It is now well established that school-based drug prevention *can* work to reduce drug consumption, at least in the short run. We emphasize *can* because large sums of money are still poured into programs whose effectiveness is dubious. However, there are proven models available for implementation.

Most successful drug prevention programs are not targeted to specific substances. Which drugs, then, do they affect? Besides differing in the legality of their use, drugs differ in the cost burden they place on society. Where are the benefits of a drug prevention program realized? Through a reduction in crime related to the cocaine market? Through fewer traffic accidents and higher productivity associated with lower alcohol use? Or through less money spent caring for the health of smokers? To put the question more provocatively, are school-based drug prevention programs better viewed as a weapon in the "war" against illegal drugs or as a public health program for decreasing the adverse effects of licit substances?

The answers to such questions will give both policymakers and the public a clearer understanding of the merits of school-based drug prevention programs and limit unrealistic expectations. Those answers also bear on who should be funding drug prevention and what types of programs prevention should be competing against for scarce resources. In this book, we identify where drug prevention's benefits fall—in reductions in the use of illicit drugs, drinking, or smoking. And we determine whether all these benefits combined exceed the costs of running the prevention programs.

Our estimates are limited to tangible, measurable benefits. Those benefits include reduced productivity losses due to death, incarceration, and victimization from crime, but not illness, and also reductions in the costs of health care, the criminal justice system, and the social-welfare system. We omit certain benefits such as reductions in pain and suffering and loss of life, the quantification of which is difficult and controversial. Our estimates apply to a hypothetical drug prevention program that is representative of real-world programs that have been shown to be successful. We do not evaluate specific programs separately or recommend one program over another.

CENTRAL FINDINGS

To answer the broadest question of this study—do the benefits of school-based drug prevention programs outweigh their costs?—we conclude that the benefits of model programs do in fact exceed the costs. According to the best estimate we can now make (see Figure S.1), society (i.e., the United States as a whole)[1] realizes total quantifiable benefits of $840 from one average student's participation in drug prevention at this mature stage of the U.S. drug epidemic. By comparison, the cost of one student's participation comes to $150. Long-term benefits are always difficult to estimate, and our benefit estimate is subject to a number of assumptions—e.g., how effective a program can be, how the effects decay, and how much of a substance would be consumed without the program. All of our assumptions are uncertain to some degree. We randomly and repeatedly varied our assumptions across reasonable ranges of values to generate a large set of possible total benefit measures. About 95 percent of the time, the benefits exceeded $300—twice the amount of the costs.

Both our best and our conservative benefit estimates account for school-based prevention's effects on only four drugs—alcohol, tobacco, marijuana, and cocaine. These are the four drugs for which

---

[1]Our analysis uses data on U.S. programs and social costs, but our general conclusions may also be of interest to people in other countries.

the evidence supported the estimates of the magnitude of lifetime reductions in use. If one were to assume that prevention programs reduce the use of other illicit drugs (heroin, methamphetamines, and other controlled substances) by the same proportion that they reduce cocaine use, the estimated benefits per participant would rise to about $1,000.

Which drugs account for most of prevention's benefits? Close to 40 percent of the social value of drug use prevention is realized through reductions in tobacco use, and over a quarter of the value is in decreased alcohol abuse. Most of the remaining third is associated with reductions in cocaine, and marijuana accounts for a very small fraction of the total.

Even if we assume that prevention reduces use of other illicit drugs (such as heroin and methamphetamines) by as much as it reduces cocaine use, it is still the case that roughly two-thirds of the quantifiable social benefits from drug use prevention are due to reductions in the use of legal drugs—alcohol and tobacco. (See Figure S.2.) It therefore makes more sense to view prevention principally as a public-health program with incidental benefits in the war on (illicit) drugs rather than viewing it principally as a criminal justice intervention in the war on drugs.

IMPLICATIONS OF THE FINDINGS

What do these findings mean for taxpayers funding school-based drug prevention? First, the benefit estimates of which we are most confident suggest that model drug use prevention programs can be justified on a benefit-cost basis by reductions in substance use. Even a conservative estimate of prevention's total benefits suggests that the social gains from prevention justify its costs twice over. Drug prevention thus appears to be a wise use of public funds, at least for those patient enough to value benefits accruing some years in the future. Whether it is the wisest use of public funds depends on whether there are other uses of those funds that could reap even greater social benefits. That subject is beyond the scope of this report.

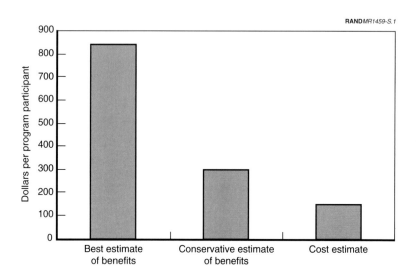

Figure S.1—Estimate of Social Benefits Versus Cost of School-Based Drug Prevention

Because at least two-thirds of prevention's benefits fall within the public-health arena, as opposed to the illicit-drug-control arena, some might infer from this discussion that prevention should be viewed as a public health intervention, and not a criminal justice intervention. The implication might then be that school-based drug prevention should be funded out of health dollars rather than criminal justice (or education) dollars. Indeed, there is some merit in this observation. Certainly, it would be foolish not to fund drug prevention simply because law enforcement interventions are seen as a higher priority for scarce criminal justice program dollars when public-health or education funding streams are available.

Concerns over the source of budgetary support for school-based drug prevention programs should not obscure the fact that the dominant costs of running these prevention programs are not dollar costs (e.g., for purchasing program materials). Rather, the dominant cost is from the students' lost learning opportunity, which is the re-

RAND*MR1459-S.2*

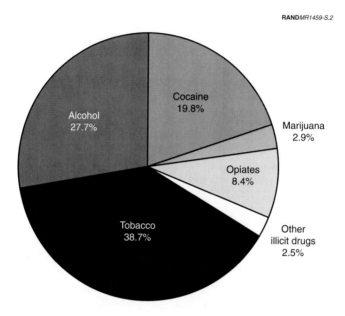

Figure S.2—Source of Drug-Related Prevention Benefits

sult of diverting scarce class time from traditional academic subjects into drug prevention instruction. Unless the school year is lengthened to compensate for the time diverted to drug prevention—an unlikely prospect—the principal social cost of drug prevention will be the displacement of equivalent time spent on education in traditional subjects.

Although drug prevention is a wise use of public funds, that is mainly because drug prevention is relatively cheap and because drug use is so costly to society, and not because even model programs eliminate a large proportion of drug use. In fact, our best estimates are that prevention reduces lifetime consumption of tobacco by 2.3 percent, lifetime abuse of alcohol by 2.2 percent, and lifetime use of cocaine by 3.0 percent. Yet, even such small reductions in use can cause large decreases in social cost. And small reductions are all that anyone should expect from prevention. Communities should not undertake drug prevention with the hope that they will see striking declines in the rate of overall drug use, or even noticeable declines. Prevention is a cost-effective tool for improving the public health and for making *incremental* progress in efforts to manage a mature drug epidemic, such as the cocaine use epidemic in the United States.

CONCEPTUAL FRAMEWORK

This study's findings and implications rest on a methodology that is simple in broad outline. The resulting estimates of the benefits versus the costs of school-based drug prevention programs, graphed in Figure S.1, are expressed in terms of dollars' worth of social cost averted per prevention program participant. As the figure clearly shows, the benefits from school-based drug prevention are probably several times as great as the costs. Cost averted per participant is obtained by multiplying together three aggregate factors: the amount of substance consumed in an average participant's lifetime, the percentage reduction in lifetime consumption associated with prevention, and the social cost per unit of substance consumed (that is, if lifetime consumption is measured in grams, then social cost is in dollars per gram). These three aggregate factors are themselves the products of other factors.

Estimating the three aggregate factors is not simple or straightforward. However, in the case of the first and last factors, the complexities are technical matters of extracting pertinent numbers from data that are subject to various limitations. Estimating the middle factor, prevention-related reduction in lifetime drug use, is not free of technical challenges but is also characterized by issues that lie closer to the core of how prevention works. The derivation of that factor thus deserves further attention, which it receives in this report.

The raw material for the estimation consists of results from the evaluations of seven effective drug prevention programs (see Appendix C for a description of those programs). To our knowledge, these are the only programs to have demonstrated, with sufficient scientific rigor, to have reduced drug consumption among adolescents. The effects—typically measured in terms of impact on initiation of drug use—generally decay entirely by the end of high school. That does not mean that effectiveness is limited to the early adolescent years. Rather, later initiation has been shown to be strongly correlated with lower lifetime consumption. We thus use these correlations to predict lifetime use reductions from the measured short-term initiation effects. In doing so, we consider variation across evaluations in end-of-program effectiveness, variant forms of decay (linear or not), and the possibility that our assumptions of total decay by the end of high school may be too conservative. Thus, we also estimate reasonable ranges for the values of various factors (although for simplicity's sake, we emphasize our best estimates in this summary); those reasonable ranges are inputs for the "Conservative Estimate of Benefits" in Figure S.1.

Further qualifications and adjustments are necessary before we arrive at a best estimate of the percentage effect of prevention on lifetime drug consumption. What we want to stress here, though, is that all of the components of the overall calculation of benefits are in the form of factors to be multiplied together. This multiplicative framework should facilitate further investigation of prevention's benefits.

If further research suggests that certain inputs to the calculation should be altered, or if another analyst's or another reader's judgment differs from ours, the factor in question can simply be adjusted accordingly. Thus, if it is judged that our estimate of the social cost saved per gram of cocaine not consumed should be only two-thirds of what we claim it is, that factor can be reduced by a third, and the total benefit from cocaine use reduction would then also be reduced by a third. We consider this transparent estimation model to be one of the key contributions of this research.

ACKNOWLEDGMENTS

We are grateful to the Robert Wood Johnson Foundation for its continued sponsorship of research on the costs and benefits of drug control strategies. One of us (Rosalie Pacula) received additional support for her work on the social costs of drug use from the National Institute on Drug Abuse. Preparation and production of the final text was funded by RAND's Drug Policy Research Center through its core funding from The Ford Foundation.

Susan Everingham of RAND and Gernot Tragler of the Vienna University of Technology provided very thorough and helpful reviews. This book has benefited substantially from their comments. We also thank Nancy DelFavero of RAND for her careful editing of the final report.

We are much indebted to our late colleague Peter Rydell, who inspired our research on modeling the effectiveness of drug control interventions.

Chapter One

INTRODUCTION

Drug prevention, like motherhood and apple pie, has few opponents. Most people are instinctively supportive of using education programs to "save our kids" from addiction. Nevertheless, it is appropriate and sensible to ask whether these programs actually work. For many years, there was little solid evidence on the affirmative side. Over the past 15 years, however, compelling evidence from rigorously conducted evaluations has repeatedly shown that the better school-based programs—although by no means all programs—yield tangible effects, often across a variety of substances.

ARE PREVENTION'S EFFECTS LARGE ENOUGH TO BE WORTH THE EFFORT?

In scientific parlance, "statistically significant" differences have been found between "treatment" groups that receive prevention intervention and "control" groups that do not on a variety of outcome measures, such as knowledge and attitudes about drugs and even self-reported drug use behavior.

The next logical question to ask is whether these differences that are "statistically significant" are also "practically significant." If one uses a large enough sample and fine enough measurements, differences can be reliably detected that are so small as to be of little practical significance. Might then prevention's effects be real but irrelevant? This question is inherently difficult to answer because some of the most important outcomes, e.g., injection drug use or addiction to expensive drugs such as cocaine and heroin, occur with a lag (initiation of these behaviors typically occurs in the late teens and early 20s) and are difficult to measure. Drawing inferences about those outcomes from more-proximate and readily observed outcomes, such as survey responses of ninth-graders, is necessarily a somewhat inexact science dependent upon extrapolation. Nevertheless, a few studies have adopted this sort of "benefit-cost" or "policy analytic" approach. Those studies tend to conclude that school-based prevention's effects are large enough to make the effort worthwhile. In other words, the dollar value of averted drug use exceeds the cost of running the prevention program. The policy recommendation stemming from this finding is that prevention programs are a *good investment* and society is well advised to fund them.

"Society" is not, however, a monolithic decisionmaker. Because we are not governed by a mythical "benevolent dictator" or social planner, this finding begs the question: Who in particular should fund prevention? The answer is not that obvious because prevention programs can generate a diverse set of benefits that fall within the domain of many different governmental agencies or funding streams. Programs that reduce substance use can also improve educational attainment, reduce criminal involvement, discourage precocious sexual activity, and encourage physical fitness in general. These benefits are of interest to a state's departments of education, health, public welfare, corrections, police, and juvenile justice, among others, as well as to local and federal authorities.

The issue of characterizing the distribution of benefits has not been fully addressed by the studies that conclude prevention is a good investment because those studies typically have focused on a single category of benefits. When the benefits of prevention in just one area exceed the program costs, the results have clearly justified the value of prevention. Researchers in these studies can therefore avoid having to collectively estimate outcomes as diverse as improvement of high school completion rates and reduction of marijuana use, for example.

BACKGROUND AND GOALS OF THIS STUDY

This book is the latest in a series from RAND's Drug Policy Research Center on the benefits and costs of different approaches to controlling drug consumption. It is the second report in the series on school-based prevention; the first (Caulkins et al., 1999) focused on cocaine and drew on evaluation results from two prevention programs. We now take advantage of data from additional programs. (We are not interested in comparing programs in this report, but in synthesizing results to determine what a typical effective drug prevention program might achieve.)

We were able to use more-sophisticated analytic methods than we used in the past, and here we expand beyond our focus on cocaine to analyze in equal detail the effects that school-based prevention programs have on the use of other drugs. We continue, however, with our approach of quantifying and valuing prevention's benefits by extrapolating from short-term reductions in self-reported use during the school years to long-term decreases over an entire life span.

We also take a step toward describing the distribution of prevention's benefits. It is a small step, but it is one we think will be of particular interest to policymakers and the public generally. We estimate the degree to which prevention benefits society through its effects on the use of illicit drugs such as marijuana and cocaine, as opposed to its effects on the use of licit substances such as alcohol and tobacco. Is prevention principally a weapon in the "war" on illicit drug use, with incidental benefits in the way of reductions in alcohol or cigarette use? Or does it exert its principal effects through reductions in alcohol and cigarette use? That is, should it more properly be viewed as a tool in the public health arsenal, with incidental effects on illicit drugs? Such questions are important because they bear on the issue of who should fund prevention and what types of programs prevention should be competing against for limited resources.

The Office of National Drug Control Policy (ONDCP)[1] construes prevention to be an integral part of its strategy to reduce the consumption of illicit substances, along with border interdiction, drug treatment, and domestic law enforcement. The ONDCP's goals include reducing juvenile smoking and drinking because they are illegal activities for youth and because they are significant risk factors in predicting subsequent use of marijuana and harder drugs. Preventing

---

[1]The policy discussions in this book are most relevant to the United States, and our quantitative estimates of benefits and costs are based on U.S. data; nevertheless, our general conclusions may also be of interest to people in other countries.

alcohol and cigarette consumption by adults, however, is not part of the ONDCP's agenda; therefore, resulting benefits are not included in the ONDCP's considerations regarding the proper allocation of funds among prevention, treatment, and enforcement activities.

In contrast, some in the public health community tend to emphasize the benefits of drug prevention in reducing the consumption of licit substances, pointing to the fact that use of tobacco and alcohol kills many more people annually than does the consumption of illicit drugs. As Kleiman (1992) notes, such a comparison is unfair because the mortality figures for alcohol and tobacco use are more inclusive—they include mortality associated with chronic and indirect consequences—than are the figures for illicit drugs, which generally include only acute overdose deaths as reported by medical examiners. Nevertheless, the basic point remains that smoking and alcohol abuse directly affects more than 50 million Americans whereas the number addicted to illicit substances is probably below 5 million. So, from a public health perspective, it is easy to understand why one would think of drug prevention in terms of reductions in the consumption of licit substances, with reductions in illicit drug use viewed as welcome bonuses.

If the principal benefits of drug prevention programs stem from reductions in illicit drug use, then it makes sense to compare those programs with other programs for controlling illicit drugs, such as crop eradication in source countries. It may also make sense to have these programs compete for funds from the same source. If, however, the principal benefits stem from reductions in alcohol and tobacco use, then it makes more sense to fund prevention programs from other sources, such as from the proceeds of the so-called global tobacco settlement. In this case, drug prevention would be competing against other health-related uses of such funds, such as cancer research.

OUR APPROACH: ITS STRENGTHS AND WEAKNESSES

We are interested in the effects of school-based prevention programs on lifetime substance use. To directly measure the lifetime effects of prevention on substance use, we would need to conduct an experiment. Such an experiment would entail recruiting a representative sample of children and randomly assigning some to prevention programs while keeping the others out. Both groups would then have to be tracked for 30 years or more with periodic questionnaires about drug use and various social measures such as health, employment, and criminal activity. Unfortunately for scientific rigor, this kind of experiment presents design and implementation challenges, from both practical and ethical standpoints. Nor has history provided us with a "natural experiment" in which today's cutting-edge prevention programs were applied to a random subset of people who have now completed their substance use. So, if we are going to ground our analysis in a rigorous controlled evaluation, we must mathematically extrapolate from some intermediate measurable effects to infer what those effects suggest for changes in lifetime consumption.

The Mathematical Model

Mathematical models and extrapolation are inexact and depend on various assumptions ranging from whether drugs will be more or less popular in the future to the length of a typical career of drug use. We respond to this imprecision and dependence on assumptions in two ways:

- First, for each model parameter, we test a wide range of plausible values and focus on qualitative conclusions that are robust with respect to reasonable variations within these ranges. That is, we make quantitative estimates of reductions in substance use, but we are concerned less with whether a number is 48 or 51 than we are with the broad qualitative conclusion that the number supports, e.g., that prevention saves more than it costs.

- Second, we structure the model as a series of multiplicative factors, rather than as a mysterious "black box" that spits out bottom-line numbers but gives readers no intuitive sense of how those numbers were generated. We structured these multiplicative factors and derived their baseline values in such a way that readers who disagree with some of our assumptions can plug in their own values for the relevant parameters and derive their own conclusions. Thus, rather than providing only a single numerical answer, we seek to provide an intellectual framework for understanding the issues being addressed. Unlike most intellectual frameworks, however, this one is quantitative, not qualitative, and it permits the reader to implement the framework with specific numerical estimates.

Data Sources

We built the intellectual framework primarily from three sources of empirical evidence:

1. Experimental evaluations of school-based prevention programs

2. Surveys of drug use in the general population

3. And, for certain parameters, other published research.

Among the thousands of evaluations of prevention interventions, we focus on the most rigorous ones. This allows us a high degree of confidence in the accuracy of prevention's short-term effects as measured not long after completion of a program. Nonetheless, even the soundest evaluations are subject to uncertainty in the effect estimates that are generated, and this uncertainty is propagated in our use of these estimates.

A significant threat to the validity of experimental evaluations of prevention programs is that they rely heavily on self-report measures, such as self-reports of whether respondents have ever tried marijuana. The researchers who conduct these evaluations take every reasonable step to enhance the quality of these self-report data (ensuring anonymity, checking for inconsistent patterns of answers, and even in some cases taking biological samples from respondents). Nevertheless, some respondents may lie, either to mask actual use (e.g., out of fear of possible punishment) or to embellish levels of use (e.g., to impress peers).

A second limitation concerning data from these well-run experimental evaluations is simply their lack of comparability. Different programs operate over different time periods, use different measures of short-term effects, are tested in different populations, and differ in other ways. In synthesizing the results of the various program evaluations to represent what is typical of effective programs, we therefore must make numerous ad hoc decisions regarding which specifications to choose as representative and how to figure in the results of programs with different specifications. While we regard these as reasonable decisions, they are nevertheless subject to uncertainty, and we attempt to measure their potential effects on our conclusions.

The third and perhaps most-fundamental limitation of the evaluations of prevention's short-term impact is that very little evidence is available about the persistence of effects. We have good measures of the impact on use during and immediately after a prevention program, and in most cases the short-term effects have decayed by the twelfth grade (although there could be longer-term ramifications). However, there is disappointingly little evidence concerning the rate of decay. Do the effects dissipate very quickly, meaning that there is little effect not only by the twelfth grade but also by the tenth and eleventh grades, or are there significant effects through the tenth and eleventh grades that disappear just before final data collection in twelfth grade? Therefore, we simply posit multiple plausible "scenarios" (see Chapter Four) and carry through the calculations for each because there simply is not adequate evidence to anoint one or the other as the most favored.

The second major source of data is surveys of drug use in the general population, specifically the National Household Survey on Drug Abuse (NHSDA). It is essentially the only publicly available source of information concerning illicit drug use by the general population, including use beyond young adulthood. Hence, there is really no alternative to the NHSDA despite its significant limitations. The single greatest limitation is that the NHSDA misses a large amount of, indeed in some cases the majority of, drug use, particularly for illicit drugs. Some illicit drug use is overlooked because people fall outside the NHSDA's sample frame or simply refuse to participate, and there is every reason to believe that hard-core addicts are disproportionately represented among such people. Some drug use is missed simply because the NHSDA, like most prevention evaluation studies, relies on self-reporting. Our fundamental response to this problem is to use the NHSDA only to estimate percentages of reductions in use, not reductions in actual quantities used. If prevention affects use that is *not recorded* in the NHSDA to the same degree that it affects use that *is recorded* in the NHSDA, then our answers will not be biased. Unfortunately, there is no way to validate that assumption.[2]

One may wonder why we even need data on drug use later in life if prevention's effects have already decayed by the twelfth grade. This need is best explained by example: Imagine a prevention program that reduces marijuana use during the program (say, in the sixth through eighth grades) and immediately afterward (in the ninth grade), but by the twelfth grade, lifetime prevalence of marijuana use in the treatment group has risen to that of the control group. Effectively, this means that prevention delayed initiation into marijuana use for some youth until the later grades, e.g., from the sixth through ninth grades to the eleventh or twelfth grade. We know from historical data that there is a strong correlation between age of first marijuana use and total lifetime use of marijuana. Those who start using marijuana at a younger age tend to use more of it and for a longer period of time. There is a similar relationship between age of marijuana initiation and lifetime cocaine use. So knowing that prevention has delayed initiation gives one grounds for optimism that it may also reduce lifetime use.

Unfortunately, although there is reason to be optimistic, there is no guarantee that delayed initiation also reduces lifetime use. It is possible that when prevention programs delay youths' initiation into marijuana use, those youths end up using no less marijuana than they would have in the absence of prevention. In other words, would-be seventh-grade initiates whose drug use is delayed by prevention until the twelfth grade may differ from youths who would not have started using marijuana until the twelfth grade even if they were not exposed to any prevention program. One who is optimistic about long-term prevention effects would say that these two groups of youths are not the same on every dimension; however, if both early initiation and subsequent drug use are driven by some underlying and unobserved predisposition, the two groups may be the same with respect to that predisposition. A skeptic would say that mari-

---

[2]An example of a threat to the validity of this assumption would be if those who are resistant to prevention programming would underreport drug use to a greater extent than would those who are more easily influenced by prevention programs.

juana use in one's teen years and drug use in one's 20s might be driven by completely different mechanisms. Changing the first might have no effect on the second.

One of the fundamental limitations of our analytical approach is that the only way we can build a bridge between observed changes in use during high school and projected changes in lifetime use is to rely on the historical correlations we just described, even though we acknowledge that the skeptics who say that high school and lifetime use have different drivers may have a point. In the spirit of transparency, we carry through the calculations from the optimist's perspective, but then explicitly include a multiplier (called the *correlation/causation qualifier*) whose sole purpose is to reflect the extent to which the skeptic might be right. In our baseline analysis, we set this multiplier to be 0.9, suggesting that the optimist's view is basically correct, but giving some small weight to the skeptic's views. (Readers who favor a different balance can simply substitute their own values for this multiplier. By design, individual opinion with respect to this particular factor has no impact whatsoever on any of the other factors or calculations in our analysis.)

The final source of data for our analysis consists of studies of certain parameter values. For example, the literature supports the view that the social costs associated with tobacco use in the United States are on the order of $100 billion per year. We do not derive figures such as this. We simply cite the source literature for the figure and insert it into our overall policy analysis. The fact that we can find such figures in the literature does not, however, mean that they are any less vulnerable to imprecision or inaccuracy than are the numbers that we derive ourselves. For example, there is an energetic discussion about how to assign a social cost to premature death caused by tobacco smoking. Should that valuation be higher for someone who is highly skilled and makes a lot of money than for someone else who does not possess skills that are valued so greatly in the labor market? In such cases, we point out the strengths and limitations of these parameters we borrowed from the literature, but we are doing nothing more than plugging into our calculations the figure that best represents the consensus of the literature, to the extent that any consensus exists.

By now, it should be clear that current sources of information do not permit certain, precise answers. We undertake this exercise with the belief that a reasonable, approximate answer to an important question is of at least as much interest as a highly precise answer to a technical question with no direct bearing on a policy decision. It is also at least as valuable as adopting the intellectually honest but unhelpful position of remaining noncommittal with respect to all complex questions and, hence, practically all real-world decisions and problems.

ORGANIZATION OF THIS REPORT

In the following chapters, we present the results of our analysis at increasing levels of detail. We begin in Chapter Two by presenting our principal results regarding the social benefits and costs of prevention for each of the drugs being examined and an analysis of the robustness of our results—how well the results stand up to changes in our assumptions. We also present our best-guess and conservative estimates for each of the ten factors on which our results rest. Chapter Two ends with our conclusions from this study and a general discussion of the significance of our findings. Chapters Three through Seven expand on our determination of the values for the ten factors. The appendices offer further details regarding the methodologies for calculating some of those factors.

SOCIAL BENEFIT AND COST RESULTS

In this chapter, we present our principal findings and conclusions, which we expand upon in the chapters that follow. We begin by laying out a ten-factor model by which we calculate the social benefits of school-based drug prevention. We then give our best-guess estimates of the social benefits and costs, allocated by type of drug, and supplement those best-guess estimates with a very conservative estimate. We then give an analysis of the sensitivity of our best-guess estimates to variation in our assumed factor values. Finally, we draw policy-related conclusions and offer a general discussion of our findings.

HOW WE ESTIMATE PREVENTION'S SOCIAL BENEFITS

Drug use generates social costs in terms of increased health care, lost productivity, and other costs. The social value or social benefit of a drug use prevention program includes the social costs that would have been incurred without the program.[1] Estimating the social costs of drug use is thus an important part of estimating prevention's social benefit. Prevention itself also has a social cost in terms of the resources used in administering the program; we address this issue later in this chapter.

---

[1] Prevention programs may also have positive effects on behavior beyond reduction in drug use. For example, they may contribute to higher educational attainment or broader health-promoting behaviors. We do not attempt to account for such benefits.

We begin the calculation of prevention's social benefit by estimating how much of a drug (e.g., how many grams of cocaine) the average person would use over the course of a lifetime. We then estimate by what percentage we would expect a model prevention program to reduce that usage. Multiplying those two estimates gives us the reduction in use (e.g., the number of grams of cocaine not used) by the average person exposed to the prevention program. We can then multiply that number by a social value that reflects the social costs averted per a given amount of drug not used. The resulting equation is: *Social value per amount of drug use averted* times *total amount of drug use averted* equals *total social value*. The figures for various substances can be compared to get a sense of the drugs for which the reductions are most valuable. Likewise, the sum of these figures across drugs can be compared with the cost of running a prevention program to get a sense of whether that program is likely to be a good investment.

Thus, to calculate social benefit, we make three estimates: *amount of use, percentage reduction in use,* and *social value per unit of drug not used.* We cannot estimate the first two numbers directly, however, because they are the products of two and three other factors, respectively. Furthermore, there are several *adjustments* that must be made to the estimated reduction in use, principally to more closely align that estimate with what we know about how prevention programs work in the real world. Those adjustments add another four factors. Including the factor for social value per unit of drug not used, we thus come up with a ten-factor model for calculating social benefit, as shown in Table 2.1.

In the following sections, we describe each of the ten factors and give some sense of how they were estimated. We numbered each factor from 1 to 10, and will refer to those factors by number in the remainder of this report. Table 2.1 also notes where each factor is discussed in more depth.

Lifetime Drug Use per Person in the Absence of Prevention

What we eventually want from our model is an estimate of lifetime social benefits per person participating in a prevention program. To arrive at that estimate, we first need to estimate reductions in life-

Table 2.1

Factors Used in Calculating Social Benefit from Reduction in Drug Use over a Lifetime

Factor Number	Factors for Each Estimate Used in Calculating Social Benefit	Discussed Further in Chapter . . .
	Lifetime Drug Use per Person in the Absence of Prevention	
1	Use per initiate in the absence of prevention	Three
2	Proportion of cohort who would initiate in the absence of prevention	Three
3	Discount factor	Three
	Percentage Reduction in Lifetime Use Expected from Prevention	
4	Percentage reduction in predictor of use observed at end of prevention program	Four
5	Percentage reduction in lifetime use per unit reduction in predictor at end of program	Five
	Adjustments to Reduction in Use	
6	Correlation/causation qualifier	Six
7	Scale-up qualifier	Six
8	Social multiplier	Six
9	Market multiplier	Six
	Social Cost per Unit of Use	
10	Social cost per unit of use	Seven

time use. Prevention program effectiveness is usually expressed in terms of percentage reductions in use, so we need to find the base to which such reductions should be applied. That is, we need an estimate of lifetime drug use per person in the absence of prevention. To estimate drug consumption per person, we estimate drug consumption per user and multiply it by the percentage of the population that at some point in their lives initiate drug use. We do this calculation (for the following two factors and all other factors) for each of the four drugs of principal interest: cocaine, marijuana, alcohol, and tobacco.

Factor 1: Use per Initiate in the Absence of Prevention. For cocaine, we use the estimate developed for the Drug Policy Research Center's earlier study of prevention (Caulkins et al., 1999). In that study, three approaches were used to generate six estimates of lifetime cocaine consumption. From the distribution of these numbers, a mid-range estimate was inferred. For the other three drugs (marijuana, alcohol, and tobacco), we also used three estimation approaches for each, and we averaged the results of the three approaches. The first approach for the other three drugs is one we also used to estimate co-caine consumption—an aggregate estimate in which we simply take some lengthy period of time and divide total drug use over that period by the number of people initiating use of that drug during that period. The other two approaches use individual-level data from the National Household Survey of Drug Abuse (NHSDA). The second approach involves multiplying the amount that the average drug user consumes at each age by the probability of using at that age (given that the person uses at some point in his or her life) and summing all the products over the life span of the user. The third approach involves constructing a lifetime profile of consumption for each drug-user survey respondent. This approach permits an estimate of lifetime consumption for each such respondent, and these estimates are averaged.[2]

Factor 2: Proportion of Cohort Who Would Initiate in the Absence of Prevention. For all four drugs, we determine the probability that a respondent to the NHSDA has been a user by the time that respondent has reached his or her current age (as Caulkins et al. [1999] did for cocaine alone). The probability typically is low for very young children and rises rapidly for people in their late teens and 20s (the precise timing of the rise in use depends on the drug). For the illicit drugs, the probability of a person ever having used drugs slowly falls back toward zero for persons of older ages (i.e., people born early in the 20th century). This drop-off is due to older people having passed through what would have been their peak initiation years before marijuana and cocaine use became widespread. We use these data and what we know about drug use trends to infer what seems to us to be likely estimates of this factor for current cohorts of youth.

Factor 3: Discount Factor. It is customary in social policy analyses to recognize that people, including policymakers and taxpayers, generally like to receive their benefits as soon as possible and to defer

---

[2]These estimates (except the estimate for alcohol) correct for underreporting in the NHSDA. They do not correct for the effect of any prevention program to which users may have been exposed in the past. Few of the prevention efforts offered in the past, however, have been very effective, so our absence of a discussion of past prevention programs here and elsewhere in this book may be taken as shorthand for "absence of effective prevention." Alcohol estimates are not adjusted for underreporting because the unit of consumption itself is defined in terms of self-reported instances of a behavior.

costs as long as possible. Specifically, one typically discounts future-year outcomes back to the present at some annual discount rate, such as 4 percent, in real terms. However, for this analysis, we do not have the product of Factors 1 and 2 as a stream of annual values; we have them just as a single total. Thus, we separately obtain the relationship between present discounted value and the undiscounted future stream and express that relationship as a discount factor—discounted value divided by undiscounted value. That discount factor can be multiplied by Factors 1 and 2 to yield the present value of expected future consumption by the average program participant in the absence of prevention.

Percentage Reduction in Lifetime Use Expected from School-Based Prevention

The effectiveness of school-based prevention programs on lifetime drug use has not been directly measured. It is not practical to track program participants for such a long time nor has enough time passed since the first successful prevention programs were undertaken. Most evaluations have not included even midterm follow-ups of five or ten years that may have yielded valuable data. National surveys *have* asked drug users about the amounts of drugs they have used and about early indicators of drug use,[3] so that correlations can be established between these indicators and lifetime use. We thus begin the discussion of the following two factors with the results from evaluations of prevention programs indicating effectiveness in terms of early predictive measures of subsequent drug use. We then use the correlations between the early indicators of drug use and lifetime use to convert short-term effects into estimates of lifetime consumption effects.

Factor 4: Percentage Reduction in Predictor of Use Observed at End of Prevention Program. Various evaluations have measured the success of model prevention programs at reducing marijuana,

---

[3]These indicators are "hard" numbers—for example, the age at which substance use (or frequent substance use) is initiated—not attitudinal indicators, which are less likely to be reliably recalled in later surveys, such as the NHSDA.

alcohol, and tobacco use over the short term.[4] We aggregate these measurements across programs to derive a single number for each drug that expresses the effect on the indicator or predictor value— typically probability of initiation to date—as of the end of a typical model program, which occurs at about the eighth grade.

Factor 5: Percentage Reduction in Lifetime Use per Unit Reduction in Predictor at End of Program. To translate reductions in initiation at the end of a program into reductions in lifetime use, we use three steps:

1. We estimate the amount by which the effect on initiation decays each year through age 18.

2. For those whose initiation was delayed by prevention, we account for the duration of that delay. In our "best guess" conservative scenario, which we discuss later in this report, we assume that all students whose initiation is delayed by middle-school prevention initiate before the end of high school. The result of these first two steps is a series of initiation probabilities by age following the end of the program. We also know from survey data what the probabilities are in the absence of prevention.

3. We use data from the same survey to establish correlations between the value of the short-term predictor at each age, with and without the program, and eventual use of each drug. From the correlations, we directly obtain the differences in eventual use between program participants and nonparticipants, expressed as percentages (see Chapter Five for more information). These percentages are what we want Factors 4 and 5, taken together, to yield: a percentage reduction for each drug, which we can then multiply by lifetime use to get the amount of lifetime use reduced or averted—e.g., grams not consumed or cigarettes not smoked.

We do not need a Factor 5 figure to arrive at these results, but we calculate it anyway (by dividing the results by Factor 4) to sustain the integrity and utility of the ten-factor multiplicative model. Factor 5 is therefore the percentage reduction in lifetime use achieved for every 1 percent reduction in predictive effect observed at program's end.

---

[4]For cocaine, there is insufficient short-term (school-age) use to support an effectiveness measure. Instead, we relate long-term cocaine use to short-term marijuana use.

Adjustments to Reduction in Use

Of the four adjustments we make to estimated reduction in use, two are qualifiers—numbers less than 1 that reflect our uncertainty about whether our assumed correlated reductions will materialize as real reductions at full scale, and two are multipliers—numbers equal to or greater than 1 that reflect the likelihood that for some drugs, reduction in use by program participants will indirectly cause reduction in use by nonparticipants. These four factors are all multiplied by the reduction amount emerging from the first five factors to yield an adjusted present value of the reduction in, for example, grams of use. (For more detail on the derivation of these factors, see Chapter Six.)

Factor 6: Causation/Correlation Ratio. We initially credit prevention with having reduced the average individual's lifetime consumption by the difference between the average lifetime consumption figures for those who initiate early and those who initiate later. This assumption is justified if initiation age and lifetime use reflect some underlying predisposition to use, and prevention affects that predisposition. In effect, one can infer, by looking at the change in initiation in high school, the extent to which prevention affected that underlying (and unobservable) predisposition and extrapolate the implications of that inference to lifetime use.

However, the fact that initiation age and lifetime consumption have been highly correlated historically does not necessarily imply causality—that by changing whatever causes the first (initiation age), a prevention program will also necessarily cause a change in the second (lifetime consumption). Lifetime consumption could be determined by some other variable that is coincidentally related to initiation but is unaffected by prevention. The correlation/causation ratio is simply a factor that attenuates the effect that is estimated by the other factors to reflect this concern. By its very nature, the correlation/causation ratio is not a factor that can be calculated with any precision. Caulkins et al. (1999) used a value of 0.9 for this factor, and we adopt that figure as well.

Factor 7: Scale-Up Factor. We recognize that sometimes programs of any type, not just drug prevention programs, are less effective when implemented widely than when implemented in controlled trials. In the medical literature, this distinction is sometimes described as the difference between "efficacy" and "effectiveness," although other literatures use these terms differently. Sources of this performance degradation range from the inability to replicate the influence of a program creator's personal charisma to bureaucratic inefficiency. Scaling up a program to operational levels need not always imply degradation. Sometimes there actually can be economies of scale that lead to less degradation. But the conservative position of Caulkins et al. (1999) was that a typical experimental program might lose 40 percent of its effectiveness when reproduced widely, and we use that same figure here.

Factor 8: Social Multiplier. This multiplier reflects the fact that initiation into drug use is, in some sense, a contagious social phenomenon—e.g., one user might in turn induce two others to start to use. If this is true, then preventing the first person from using would effectively eliminate three careers of drug use, not just one; in that case, we would say the "social multiplier" was 3. Caulkins et al. (1999) analyzed a variety of epidemic models and concluded that for cocaine, in the current later stages of the U.S. epidemic, this multiplier is on the order of 2.0. To the best of our knowledge, no comparable estimates have been produced for any of the other drugs, which is not to say that their multipliers might not be greater than 1.0 or even greater than the cocaine multiplier. Nevertheless, when estimating the total social benefits of prevention, we conservatively use a figure of 1.0 for the other substances. However, when looking at the proportion of social benefit that comes from preventing the use of each of the various drugs, we set all drugs' social multipliers to the same value to avoid penalizing the substances for which studies of this factor have simply not been conducted.

Factor 9: Market Multiplier. As with Factor 8—the social multiplier— the market multiplier measures a spillover effect through which reducing one person's drug use can in turn reduce use by others. In this case, the mediating mechanism is not peer pressure or social contact but rather market supply and demand. The theory of the market multiplier is that when prevention (or treatment) reduces the demand for cocaine, existing enforcement resources become concentrated on a small market volume, increasing the effectiveness of those resources (Kleiman, 1993). The further reduction in consumption from the greater effectiveness of enforcement resources can be credited to prevention in the form of a multiplier of the benefit realized without considering the indirect market effect. Caulkins et al. (1999) estimated through a market model that this multiplier is 1.3 for cocaine. That is, for every 1.0 gram of consumption reduced directly by prevention, consumption of another 0.3 grams is reduced because more-intense enforcement drove the price up enough that the additional 0.3 grams did not sell. For marijuana, a much smaller proportion of the sellers' cost structure represents compensation for sanctions the sellers receive, and no comparable story of concentration of enforcement can be told for the licit substances. Thus, for the substances other than cocaine, we assume a market multiplier of 1.0.

Social Cost per Unit of Use

The final part of the equation in calculating the social benefit of prevention is the cost per unit of use.

Factor 10: Social Cost per Unit of Use. Substance use has many ill effects on the lives of users and, through those users, on the lives of nonusers. Some of these effects are intangible and are difficult if not impossible to quantify. Some studies have attempted estimates of a wide range of social costs of drug use, and we rely on those studies for assigning a value to this factor. These costs include health care expenditures for medical consequences and for alcohol and drug abuse services, productivity reduction associated with premature death and with crime victimization, other costs of crime, and costs of social-welfare administration. For tobacco and alcohol, drug-specific estimates of total social costs have been made (see Chapter Seven). For cocaine and marijuana, no such estimate has been made, so we derive one from an estimate of the social costs of all illicit drugs. In all cases, Factor 10 is equal to the total social cost (over the course of some period, e.g., a year) divided by the total quantity of drug consumed, over the same period.

Note: This approach assumes that the social cost associated with the marginal unit of use averted by prevention equals the average social cost per unit used. One could argue that the marginal cost is either larger or smaller than the average cost.[5]

SOCIAL BENEFIT RESULTS

Table 2.2 summarizes the results of using these ten factors to calculate social benefits for a set of parameter values that are consistent with what we would regard as a "best guess" benefit estimate. As we discuss further in later chapters, there is no one right set of parameter values because of the uncertainty and imprecision in their estimates. We present what we regard as reasonable ranges of values for each of these factors. The "best guesses" shown here represent midrange to conservative estimates.

In the table, the social benefit is shown at the bottom of each column and is the product of the ten factors listed above it. For cocaine, for example, the first three factors indicate that the present value of lifetime use without prevention for a young person today is projected to be *350 grams per user* times *0.18 users per person* times *a discount factor of 0.53* equals *33 grams per person.* According to Factors 4 and 5, prevention reduces this amount by 10.9 percent times 27.6 percent, which equals 3.0 percent, or 0.99 gram per person. The two qualifiers and the two multipliers (Factors 6 through 9) multiplied together yield 1.4, adjusting the reduction in use upward from 0.99 gram to 1.42 grams per person. Finally, consuming a gram of cocaine imposes a social cost of $215. When multiplied by 1.42 grams per person, the social benefit from reduced cocaine use per person participating in the program is about $300.[6]

---

[5]One could, in particular, argue that marginal cost is low for low quantities consumed, may increase thereafter, and then drop off again as social costs approach some upper bound. The marginal cost could thus be lower than the average (to that point) at very low quantities, higher at mid-level quantities, and lower at high quantities. If one believes that consumption of the drugs studied here is neither very low nor high by the definitions just offered, our averages underestimate marginal costs of drug use and thus the marginal value of additional prevention.

[6]Throughout this report, we round values to simplify the numbers and to emphasize that we cannot really calculate the values with the precision that several significant digits would suggest. We perform the calculations, however, with the full range of significant digits allowed by the computers we used in this study. Readers who repeat our calculations may thus get slightly different results.

Table 2.2

Best-Guess Estimates of Prevention's Impact

Factor	Cocaine	Marijuana	Tobacco	Alcohol
		Units of Use		
	Grams	Grams	Packs of Cigarettes	Self-Reported Instances of Drunkenness[a]
1: Baseline Use per Initiate	350	560	8,900	640
2: Baseline Proportion of Cohort Initiating	18%	62%	78%	58%
3: Discount Factor	0.53	0.58	0.42	0.49
4: Prevention's Short-term Effectiveness	10.9%	10.9%	16.8%	12.8%
5: Reduction in Lifetime Use per Unit of Short-Term Effectiveness	27.6%	16.0%	14.0%	17.3%
6: Correlation-Causation Ratio	0.9	0.9	0.9	0.9
7: Scale-Up Factor	0.6	0.6	0.6	0.6
8: Social Multiplier	2.0	1.0	1.0	1.0
9: Market Multiplier	1.3	1.0	1.0	1.0
10: Social Cost per Unit of Use	$215	$12	$8	$98
Social Benefit per Prevention Participant	$300	$20	$300	$210
Total		$840 per participant		

[a]We focus on drunkenness because alcohol consumption per se is not well linked to social costs. We cite self-reports because that is what our alcohol abuse estimates are based on, and we do not have a way of converting self-reports of drunkenness into actual occurrences. (Consumption numbers for other substances are adjusted for the self-reports on which they are partially based.) We tried an analogous calculation for an alternate measure of problematic alcohol consumption: self-reported instances of consuming at least five drinks at one sitting. The result was very similar: a social benefit of $180 per participant.

If we add up the Social Benefit per Prevention Participant numbers in Table 2.2, we get approximately $840 as the social benefit for one person's participation in a drug prevention program. This by no means represents the total of all benefits associated with prevention. Any benefits associated with reductions in use of other substances such as heroin, LSD, steroids, ecstasy, and so-called date-rape drugs are omitted. Those benefits are probably smaller than the benefits derived from reduced cocaine use because cocaine is associated with slightly more than half of all social costs related to illicit drugs (see

Chapter Six), but one cannot state this with certainty because the percentage reductions in use of these substances could be much greater than the percentage reductions for cocaine. We also omit the job-related productivity costs incurred by employed drug users.

Finally, prevention can bring benefits that are not related to or caused by reduced drug use, such as reduced criminal activity, reduced precocious sexual activity, increased school retention and graduation, and other such benefits. None of those benefits is included in the figure of $840 per program participant.

What quantity of drug use does prevention avert per program participant? Multiplying together the ten factors in Table 2.2 suggests that the answer is on the order of 1.42 grams of cocaine, 1.88 grams of marijuana, 36 packs of cigarettes, and 2.2 self-reported instances of getting drunk. With respect to drunkenness, self-reports are likely to be underestimates, but none of these numbers seems large. These numbers motivate two observations. First, we are averaging across all prevention program participants, and one of the drawbacks to prevention is that it is difficult to target it only to those who need it most. Thus, prevention programs are administered to many persons who would not use drugs at all or use them only occasionally. Second, as suggested by the values given for Factors 4 and 5 in Table 2.2, prevention's ultimate effects on drug use are simply not dramatic. We discuss this finding further later in this chapter.

Questions of scale aside, where does prevention make its greatest contribution? That is, how large are the benefits stemming from reductions in the use of one drug relative to the benefits stemming from reductions in the use of another drug? Some sense of this can be gained by simply reading across the second-to-last row in Table 2.2. For a fair comparison, however, we set the social multiplier for cocaine to 1.0 to make it equal to that for the other substances. The reason we did that is, as noted earlier, there is no information in the literature concerning the social multiplier for these other substances. In estimating prevention's total benefit, and the total benefit obtained through cocaine reduction, we take advantage of what we know about cocaine's social multiplier. However, in comparing across substances, there is no compelling reason a priori to suppose the social multiplier is any larger for cocaine.

Figure 2.1 shows the proportional social cost savings from prevention for the four substances (cocaine, marijuana, tobacco, and alcohol) for which we have estimates of prevention's impact. The figure
reflects the relative sizes of the savings listed in the second-to-last
row of Table 2.2 after dividing the cocaine dollar figure in half (to
eliminate its social-multiplier "bonus").

Roughly speaking, about three-quarters of the benefits we examined
are the result of prevention's effects on the use of the licit substances
(alcohol and tobacco), with effects on the latter the more important
of the two. Very little savings result from reductions in marijuana
use. Or, looking at it another way, for every $1 in savings associated
with cocaine there are about $2 in savings associated with cigarettes,
$1.40 in savings associated with alcohol, and just $0.15 in savings associated with marijuana.

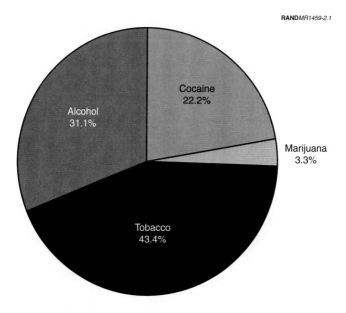

RAND*MR1459-2.1*

Figure 2.1—Relative Size of Social Cost Savings from School-Based
Prevention's Impact on the Use of Cocaine, Marijuana, Tobacco,
and Alcohol

Figure 2.1 does not imply that reductions in the use of illicit drugs account for just one-fourth of prevention's drug-related benefits because there are other illicit drugs for which the reduction in use would produce social benefits. While these other drugs are not included in our analysis, we can imagine what Figure 2.1 might look like if we assumed that prevention reduced the use of opiates and other illicit drugs other than cocaine and marijuana by the same proportion as it reduces cocaine use. We have no basis for this assumption, but prevention's effectiveness (Factor 3 times Factor 4) at reducing cocaine use is close to that for marijuana use (3.0 percent and 3.1 percent, respectively). Hence, this may not be an unreasonable approach to gaining a general impression of the proportion of prevention's benefits associated with reduced use of alcohol and tobacco versus the proportion associated with reduced use of all illicit drugs.

With this assumption, and if all the adjustments (Factors 6 through 9) are the same, the difference in social benefit realized per program participant is the result of differences in the product of Factor 1, Factor 2, and Factor 10. That product is the amount used per program participant times the social cost per amount used—in other words, the total social cost. We estimate (see Chapter Seven) that 59 percent of the social costs associated with illicit drugs are associated with cocaine, 25 percent are associated with opiates, 9 percent with marijuana, and 7 percent with other illicit drugs. Translating these estimates to Figure 2.1, we would simply scale the size of the opiates and other-illicit-drug slices of the pie to be 25/59 and 7/59 of the size of the slice for cocaine, respectively. As shown in Figure 2.2, reductions in alcohol and tobacco use would then account for two-thirds of prevention's benefits, and reductions in illicit drug use would account for one-third. The ratio of savings associated with licit to illicit drugs would thus be two to one.

SCHOOL-BASED PREVENTION'S SOCIAL COSTS

We examined program costs of school-based prevention and confirmed a basic finding of Caulkins et al. (1999). The budgetary costs (e.g., for program materials and teacher training) are very small compared with the nonbudgetary costs, in particular the opportunity cost of using school time to teach prevention rather than conventional

RAND*MR1459-2.2*

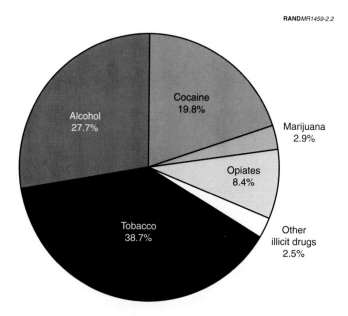

Figure 2.2—Source of Drug-Related Prevention Benefits (If Prevention Reduces Other Illicit Drug Use by as Much as It Reduces Cocaine Use)

subjects. To those responsible for allocating school district resources, it is the budgetary costs that are relevant. However, because we are interested here in social benefits, we are also interested in social costs, and those costs are not restricted to budgetary costs. The true dominant cost to society of a youth's receiving school-based drug prevention is not just the purchase price of any workbooks or posters to implement the drug prevention curriculum, or even the costs required to train the teachers. Rather, it is the loss to society from that student spending less time learning (and the teacher spending less time teaching) other more-traditional subjects.[7] This conflict is a microcosm of the much broader and intensely debated issue of whether school time should be spent providing various social ser-

_____

[7]This assumes that the prevention program is not promoting academic educational attainment. For another possibility, see the "Conclusions and Discussion" section later in this chapter.

vices and life-skills training or whether schools should focus solely on academic basics.

How much, then, is the social cost of prevention? Because the opportunity cost of the time spent on a prevention program is the principal cost driver, costs depend heavily on the number of contact hours. Effective prevention programs provide anywhere from 10 to 30 classroom hours. We chose the upper end of this range to keep our estimate of prevention's net social benefit conservative. There is considerable room for debate concerning what is the appropriate social cost to assign to a classroom contact hour because there is no market within which such hours are "traded." Caulkins et al. (1999) estimated a social cost of about $150 for a 30-session curriculum, or $5 per hour. That figure is essentially the cost of providing one student with an hour of K–12 classroom education. The presumption is that the value of education is at least as great as its cost.

Clearly, our best estimate of prevention's total social benefits ($840 per participant) is much larger than our cost estimate ($150), suggesting that *with these parameter estimates, prevention is a good social investment*. This qualification is an important one, and one to which we now turn.

SENSITIVITY OF FINDINGS TO VARIATIONS IN ASSUMPTIONS

At this point in the discussion, we have reached two fundamental findings:

1. School-based drug prevention programs generate social benefits whose dollar value exceeds the costs of running the programs.

2. School-based drug prevention may achieve important benefits by reducing the use of cocaine and opiates (in contrast to marijuana, the reduced use of which achieves limited benefits). However, the benefits associated with reduced use of licit substances are greater than, and perhaps twice as great as, the benefits associated with reduced use of all illicit substances.

Yet, the specific values of the parameters in our ten-factor model are uncertain. How robust are these two fundamental findings with respect to this uncertainty? The short answer is that the first finding is very robust, and the second is moderately robust.

With respect to the first finding, Table 2.3 reproduces Table 2.2 with values for Factors 1, 2, and 4 through 9 that are more conservative but not, we think, unreasonable.[8] With all of these parameters simultaneously at low values, the social cost savings are $43.[9]

It is thus not, at least in principle, inconsistent with our parameter ranges for the social cost of prevention to exceed the benefits. However, it is extremely unlikely that the true values of all parameters would simultaneously be at the low end of the reasonable range. To get some sense of the likelihood that the social-benefit estimate will fall below the cost estimate, we ran Monte Carlo simulations in which we randomly drew a value for each parameter from its range of values. The ranges ran from the lows (worst-case estimates) shown in Table 2.3 to a reasonable upper end exceeding the best-guess estimates shown in Table 2.2 (factor ranges are presented in Appendix A). Typically (depending on the details of the simulation),[10] about 95 percent of the trials generated benefit estimates exceeding $300 per prevention participant. Only a very few (less than 0.01 percent) produced benefit estimates below $150. So, this model and analysis suggest that it is a safe bet that the dollar-equivalent social costs avoided from reduced substance use exceed our $150 estimate of program costs.[11]

---

[8]We do not vary the discount factor because it is based on a rate that is not subject to the types of uncertainty affecting our characterization of drug use and drug markets. We also exempt Factor 10, social cost per unit of use, because we know that we are excluding important costs, so given this exclusion, it does not make sense to talk about possible variation around some best estimate.

[9]If we assume that prevention's effectiveness against illicit drugs other than cocaine and marijuana is the same as its effectiveness against cocaine, another $5.40 of benefits would be realized, bringing the total to approximately $49.

[10]We ran simulations using both uniform and triangular probability distributions. In some simulations, each parameter value was sampled independently for each drug. In others, there was some or complete correlation across drugs for particular factor values.

[11]Of course, structural (as opposed to numerical) assumptions within the model could still prove to be erroneous. For example, the legal status of one or more of the drugs may change (e.g., tobacco prohibition or cocaine legalization) within the lifetime of current youth, with undetermined effects on the benefits of prevention.

Table 2.3

Worst-Case Estimates of Prevention's Impact

Factor	Cocaine	Marijuana	Tobacco	Alcohol
			Units of Use	
	Grams	Grams	Packs of Cigarettes	Self-Reported Instances of Drunkenness
1: Baseline Use per Initiate	225	380	7,800	440
2: Baseline Proportion of Cohort Initiating	12%	53%	70%	47%
3: Discount Factor	0.53	0.58	0.42	0.49
4: Prevention's Short-term Effectiveness	4.9%	4.9%	4.3%	1.7%
5: Reduction in Lifetime Use per Unit of Short-Term Effectiveness	26.2%	15.7%	12.4%	13.2%
6: Correlation-Causation Ratio	0.5	0.5	0.5	0.5
7: Scale-Up Factor	0.5	0.5	0.5	0.5
8: Social Multiplier	1	1	1	1
9: Market Multiplier	1	1	1	1
10: Social Cost per Unit of Use	$215	$12	$8	$98
Social Benefit per Prevention Participant	$9.90	$2.70	$25.00	$5.60
Total		$43 per participant		

To address the robustness of the second finding, we ran another Monte Carlo simulation with 100,000 trials, drawing each parameter from a triangular distribution defined by its low, base, (medium) and high values. That is, we assumed the most likely values were the ones given in Table 2.2, and that probabilities of lower or higher values fell away linearly until they reached zero at the estimates given in Table 2.3 and at our most optimistic estimates (reported in Appendix A). A value was then randomly drawn from this probability distribution for each factor; the ten values then were multiplied together to yield a social benefit value. This process was repeated 100,000 times.

Not only did we vary the parameter values, we also varied our assumptions regarding the delay of initiation following prevention, i.e., whether initiation is delayed only until high school or beyond high school or whether the effect is permanent. The results presented so far, in Tables 2.2 and 2.3, are based on the conservative assumption that everyone whose initiation is delayed by middle-school drug prevention initiates drug use in high school. In this simulation, we allowed for an optimistic case, in which we assumed that initiation is delayed until ages 19 to 21. In a very optimistic case, we assumed that delayed initiators initiate with the same frequencies and at the same ages as an average 18-year-old who has not yet initiated. In the simulation, the conservative, more optimistic, and very optimistic initiation delay assumptions were equally likely.[12] The simulation results are shown in Table 2.4.

Table 2.4

Sensitivity of Benefit Distribution Across Drugs to Variations in Assumptions

	10th Percentile	Median	90th Percentile
Tobacco's share of the benefits (of four drugs)	28.2%	42.4%	56.4%
Alcohol's share of the benefits (of four drugs)	17.7%	31.8%	47.0%
Cocaine's share of the benefits (of four drugs)	12.8%	20.1%	30.3%
Marijuana's share of the benefits (of four drugs)	2.6%	4.2%	6.7%
Percentage of benefits associated with illicit drugs (of four drugs)	16.9%	24.6%	35.1%
Percentage of benefits associated with illicit drugs (including extrapolated effects on opiates and other illicit drugs)	22.4%	32.0%	44.3%
Percentage of benefits associated with licit drugs (of four drugs)	64.9%	75.4%	83.1%
Percentage of benefits associated with licit drugs (of all drugs, including extrapolated effects)	55.7%	68.0%	77.6%
Ratio of licit/illicit drug benefits (including only cocaine and marijuana)	1.85	3.07	4.93
Ratio of licit/illicit drug benefits (extrapolating to all illicit drugs)	1.26	2.12	3.47

---

[12]Similar results are obtained if the simulation includes only the conservative and more-optimistic scenarios.

Using the first row of Table 2.4 as an example, the results should be read in the following way: In half the trials, tobacco's share of the benefits associated with the four drugs we studied exceeded 42 percent, and in the other half of the trials, tobacco's share fell below that number. In 10 percent of the trials, tobacco's share fell below 28 percent, while in 90 percent of the trials, it fell below 56 percent (i.e., in the other 10 percent, it exceeded 56 percent).

The results attest to the robustness of our finding that three of the four substances analyzed here are likely to account for substantial shares of prevention's benefits. In 90 percent of the trials, prevention of tobacco use accounted for at least a quarter of the benefits from the prevention of the four drugs studied here, alcohol accounted for at least a sixth of the benefits, and cocaine accounted for at least an eighth. In contrast, marijuana accounts for more than one-fifteenth of prevention's benefits in only 10 percent of the trials. It thus seems safe to conclude that reduced marijuana use in and of itself is a secondary, not a primary, benefit of school-based drug prevention.

There is somewhat greater variation with respect to the distribution of benefits associated with licit versus illicit drugs. When considering only the four drugs studied here (cocaine, marijuana, tobacco, and alcohol), the illicit drugs (cocaine and marijuana) accounted for roughly one-quarter of the benefits. In 90 percent of the simulation trials, that share was at least one-sixth, and in 90 percent of the trials, it was no more than one-third. For those willing to assume that prevention is as effective at reducing use of opiates, amphetamines, and other illicit drugs as it is at reducing cocaine use, the presumed share of benefits associated with prevention of illicit drugs is larger, with a best guess of one-third, and shares in the one-quarter to one-half range being quite plausible.

To some extent, this finding depends on definitional issues pertaining to the social costs that are included. It might be argued, for example, that productivity losses due to premature mortality of the substance user should be excluded because that individual valued drug use over the income lost. The costs of premature mortality make up a larger portion of the social costs of tobacco and alcohol use than they do of the social costs of illicit-drug use. Thus, if one excluded productivity losses associated with premature mortality from the social cost accounting, the proportion of benefits associated with prevention of illicit drugs rises. In particular, the proportion increases to just shy of 50 percent in our base case, assuming prevention affects other illicit drugs as much as it affects cocaine use, and parameter uncertainty could easily bump up that proportion to over 50 percent.

Furthermore, two significant uncertainties not reflected in the simulation bear directly on the ratio of licit-to-illicit drug benefits. The first is the uncertainty surrounding social multipliers. In the absence of empirical evidence, we set the social multipliers to be all equal to each other, but if one substance has a social multiplier that is much higher than the others, its piece of the pie would be larger than what we depict here. Second, we really do not know that prevention has the same percentage impact on the use of illicit drugs other than cocaine that it has on the use of cocaine. So, rather than saying we are highly certain that the licit-to-illicit drug benefits ratio is at least 1.3:1 or 1.9:1 depending on which drugs are counted (see the 10th percentile results in Table 2.4), we would rather phrase the conclusion as a conditional statement.

The evidence strongly suggests that benefits associated with reduced use of licit drugs is at least as great as the corresponding benefits associated with reduced use of illicit substances, unless at least one of the following is true: (1) The social multiplier for illicit drugs is much higher than the social multiplier for licit drugs or (2) prevention is much more effective on a percentage basis at reducing heroin and other illicit drug use than it is at reducing cocaine or marijuana use.

OTHER RESULTS OF INTEREST

The quantitative analysis assembled in support of these findings included some intermediate results that are of interest in their own right—e.g., we estimated that cocaine is responsible for over half of the social costs (other than those for lost labor) associated with illicit drugs in the United States.

Likewise, we developed estimates of lifetime consumption for those who initiate. The alcohol figures are difficult to interpret because they are expressed in units of self-reported levels of use (specifically, self-reported instances of getting drunk), and the tobacco figures have no doubt been estimated elsewhere, but the marijuana figures may contribute to the literature. We estimate that, on average, people who use marijuana at least once will over their lifetime consume 375 to 875 grams of marijuana.

We also synthesized information from the best-run evaluations in the literature to estimate that a model school-based drug prevention program can be expected to cut drug use, as of the end of the program, by 4 percent to 21 percent for tobacco, 2 percent to 31 percent for alcohol, and 5 percent to 14 percent for marijuana. However, one should not expect reductions in lifetime consumption to be this large. As a rough guideline, our models suggest that reductions in lifetime use are about 15 percent as great as reductions in use observed for the relevant indicator at the completion of the program. The exception is cocaine, for which reductions in lifetime use are about 28 percent as great as the reduction in marijuana use observed at the completion of the program (as stated earlier, marijuana use is the short-term predictor for lifetime cocaine use).

CONCLUSIONS AND DISCUSSION

In this report, we show that school-based drug prevention programs are a good investment from the benefit-cost standpoint. The best estimate of social costs saved per prevention program participant ($840) greatly exceeds the program cost per participant ($150), and that dollar-figure difference is highly robust with respect to uncertainty about various parameter values.

Does this mean that these programs should be funded? Not necessarily. Other uses for the same dollars or classroom time, even other drug-related uses (such as treatment), may have even higher benefit-cost ratios. And, whether all drug-control resources should be invested in the program with the highest benefit-to-cost ratio is an issue that policymakers must resolve, while taking into account the risks from concentrating investments in drug-control in a single program.

It should also be noted that the $840 in savings does not entirely or even primarily take the form of increased revenue accruing to the government.[13] That is, we are not arguing that funding school-based prevention programs is a good way to balance the budget, even in the long run. On the other hand, a favorable social benefit-to-cost ratio is an important factor in the decision to invest in a wide range of public programs, from highway improvements to flood control. School-based drug prevention is a good social investment in that sense.

If school-based drug prevention should be funded, who should do the funding? A central finding of this book is that roughly two-thirds of drug prevention's drug-related contribution to society seems to result from reduced use of tobacco and alcohol. Benefits stemming from reductions in the use of illicit substances, while important, are smaller than the benefits from the reduction in licit substances (and the benefits from reduced use of marijuana are especially small).

Thus, school-based drug prevention's benefits do not stem primarily from reduction in the use of illicit drugs. The same cannot be said of the benefits from locking up drug dealers or some forms of drug treatment (such as methadone maintenance not accompanied by associated social services). Other forms of treatment are as much about helping addicts acquire job skills, resolve interpersonal conflicts, get help from social services, and improve their general health and welfare as they are about reducing drug use. School-based drug prevention is more akin to the other forms of treatment than it is to drug law enforcement or methadone maintenance in this regard. Although school-based drug prevention is not primarily about preventing illicit drug use, it nevertheless appears to have a favorable benefit-cost ratio on the basis of its impact on illicit drug use alone. However, viewing school-based drug prevention in so narrow a light unfairly penalizes prevention, relative to other programs for which reductions in drug use are in fact the primary benefit, because prevention's benefits with regard to licit drug use are in that case disregarded.

Some readers might infer from this discussion that school-based prevention should be viewed as a public health intervention, and not a criminal justice intervention, and thus it should be funded out of

---

[13]The data on which we based our social-cost estimates do not permit a breakdown of the savings accruing to the government versus the savings accruing to other segments of society.

health dollars rather than criminal justice (or education) dollars. Indeed, there is some merit in this observation. Certainly, it would be foolish not to fund school-based drug prevention simply because law enforcement interventions are seen as a higher priority for scarce criminal justice program dollars when public-health or education funding streams are available. That fact that such questions are even raised illustrates the fragmented nature of governmental responsibility for the public welfare. If a program does not clearly belong under one bailiwick or another, it may not be well supported by any particular element of a bureaucracy despite its broad benefits, or rather *because* of its broad benefits, since no one agency could or would claim full credit for all of the benefits.

Concerns over the source of budgetary support should not obscure the fact that the primary costs of running prevention programs are not dollar costs (e.g., for purchasing program materials). Rather, the primary cost is from the students' lost learning opportunity, which is the result of diverting scarce class time from traditional academic subjects into drug prevention instruction. Therefore, whether or not the Department of Health and Human Services, the Justice Department, the Department of Education, or some other agency subsidizes the cost of prevention program materials, the real cost will be either that the country's citizens will have 30 fewer hours of instruction on algebra and geography, or that the school day or school year will have to be extended at the expense of state and local education funding sources. It is unlikely that school days or school years will be lengthened just for the sake of those 30 hours. Thus, it appears that society in general and program participants in particular will bear the costs of school-based drug prevention by way of a slight reduction in education.

An interesting implication of the trade-off between drug prevention programs and traditional classroom instruction is that the programs should be evaluated not only in terms of their behavioral effects but also in terms of the educational value, if any, they provide. Suppose a prevention program teaches critical thinking, analysis, and writing or math skills almost as effectively as the conventional academic instruction it displaces. Such a program could be much more cost effective in a real economic sense than another prevention program that offered no such academic benefits, even if the second program were more effective at reducing drug use. Currently, drug prevention programs are rarely evaluated in terms of their contribution to educational outcomes (which are quite distinct from mere knowledge about drugs and their effects).

If, as we argue here, some two-thirds of the drug-reduction program benefits stem from reduction in licit drug use, there are implications for the development of a prevention curriculum. To a substantial degree, the materials and messages that help reduce illicit drug use also help reduce licit drug use, and vice versa, so it would be misguided to think of having to choose between a program that prevents only the use of illicit drugs and one that prevents only the use of licit drugs. However, to the extent that such conflicts could arise, it would seem unwise to make choices that reduce illicit drug use while at the same time eroding the effects on licit drug use by a comparable amount (unless the students in question were thought to have a much greater risk of illicit-drug use than the national average).

Our findings may also have implications for the level of support of drug prevention programs within schools. School administrators and teachers do not always feel comfortable with their unsought-after responsibility for helping to prevent the use of illicit drugs (Reuter and Timpane, 2001). Tying the program to a broader range of public-health benefits might serve to pique their interest.

Finally, an implication of our program effectiveness findings (see the "Other Results of Interest" section), is that prevention programs, even the cutting-edge ones, should not be viewed as "vaccines" that inoculate those in the program against drug use. There is very strong empirical support for the belief that these programs reduce drug use, but there is even stronger support for the belief that they leave an even greater proportion of baseline users unaffected. Prevention may be cost effective, but it cannot be expected to single-handedly address concerns about substance abuse, at least in its present form and as far as we currently understand prevention's effectiveness.

As a final note in that regard, one contribution that a systems analysis, such as this one, can make is to highlight those parameters for which the evidence is thinnest. In this analysis, the evidence is clearly the thinnest on the decay function. Therefore, we suggest that future evaluations of school-based drug prevention programs should plan for more frequent and sustained follow-up data collection and that researchers who have unpublished follow-up data from past evaluations should publish their results now.

In the following chapters, we expand upon our discussion of the ten factors for estimating the effects of prevention. In Chapter Three, we expand upon the discussion of Factors 1 through 3; Chapter Four further examines Factor 4; Chapter Five examines Factor 5; Chapter Six examines Factors 6 through 9; and Chapter Seven further illustrates how we estimated Factor 10.

LIFETIME DRUG CONSUMPTION WITHOUT PREVENTION

In this chapter and the following chapters, we expand upon our discussion in Chapter Two of our ten-factor model for estimating the benefits of school-based drug prevention. In this chapter, we discuss how we estimated the first three factors, which, when multiplied together, give the present value of average lifetime drug consumption per person in the absence of prevention. We begin with Factor 1—how much the average user consumes in his or her lifetime in the absence of prevention.

HOW MUCH DO USERS CONSUME OVER THEIR LIVES?

For cocaine, we adopt Caulkins et al.'s (1999) estimate that the average lifetime consumption for someone who initiates use is 350 grams, with lower and upper bounds of 225 and 475 grams, respectively. In that study, three approaches were used to generate six estimates of lifetime cocaine consumption.

The first approach called for estimating consumption by dividing total use over a period of years by the number of people who initiated use during that period. That approach yielded three estimates (457 grams, 433 grams, and 169 grams). The lowest estimate was unadjusted for use outside the period in question by those who initiated within the period, the middle estimate was adjusted for use outside the period in question, and the largest estimate took into account the number of years a cocaine consumer spent as a heavy or light user.

The second approach employed a model of the flow of users among light-use, heavy-use, and no-use categories and generated the fourth and fifth estimates. The fourth estimate (405 grams) was generated by allowing the model to run freely over users' lifetimes, and the fifth estimate (292 grams) resulted from truncating the model run to reflect lower consumption levels as users age.

The final approach generated the sixth estimate (592 grams) by dividing consumption by initiation in a single year, assuming (falsely) that cocaine use was in steady state.

The best overall estimate and the lower and upper bounds were inferred from the distribution of these six estimates and the strengths and limitations of the methods underlying them.[1]

We found no comparable estimates in the literature for marijuana, alcohol, or tobacco, so we developed our own estimates, which we use here. Because there is no single best way to estimate the values for marijuana, alcohol, and tobacco, we present three alternative approaches. We first discuss these alternatives as they apply to all three substances, then present, for each substance, the specifics of applying the methods and how the results were obtained.

Estimation Method 1: Dividing Consumption over an Historical Period by Initiation

One approach used by Caulkins et al. (1999) divided consumption over an historical period divided by initiation. A shortcoming of this approach is that (1) use during the period by those who initiated before the beginning of that period is counted in the numerator and (2) use subsequent to the end of the period by those who initiated during the period is excluded from the numerator. These "edge" effects work in opposite directions. In fact, if use during the period by prior initiates happened to exactly equal, and hence offset, future use by individuals who initiated during the period, then the estimate would not be biased. It is too much to hope that such an offset would be exact, but the longer the historical period, the less significant these

---

[1]Total population use for these estimates is not based on National Household Survey of Drug Abuse (NHSDA) reported use, and thus none of the estimates is undermined by (or uncorrected for) the underreporting in that survey.

edge effects are. Fortunately, we have data covering more than 20 years for cigarettes and 30 years for alcohol. The marijuana series of data covers a shorter time span (13 years), but the fact that the Office of National Drug Control Policy (ONDCP, 2000) reports that the number of marijuana users at the beginning of the 13-year period (11.6 million) was about the same as the number of users at the end of the period (11.7 million) is reassuring. The two edge effects are less likely to be of similar size if drug use is expanding or shrinking markedly over the period in question.

Estimation Method 2: Creating a Lifetime Profile of Consumption by Totaling Use Across Respondents of Different Ages

For Estimation Methods 2 and 3, we begin with the user-specific data from the National Household Survey on Drug Abuse (NHSDA) and estimate some measure of use (e.g., self-reported instances of getting drunk) across a user's lifetime. Method 2 uses a single year's cross-section through the NHSDA to create a lifetime profile of consumption by totaling use across respondents of different ages. Consider, for example, the hypothetical subset of NHSDA respondents' drug use profiles shown in Figure 3.1. The figure has one row for each respondent. The numbers in each row indicate the respondent's age in the year corresponding to that column; shaded boxes indicate years in which the respondent used drugs. Thus, in 1997, respondent 1 is 13, respondent 2 is 14, respondent 3 is 16, and so forth, and respondents 1 through 10, 12, and 15 used drugs. NHSDA questions focus on past-year use, so the 1997 NHSDA tells us primarily about the 1997 column only, and, of course, no survey can tell us directly about the columns at the far right that correspond to future years. So these estimation methods assume that usage by respondents who are, say, 16 in 1997 represents usage by all respondents in whatever year they were or will be 16.

We compute expected lifetime consumption per man who ever initiated and per woman who ever initiated by summing across all ages the amount consumed at each age. The amount used at some age by the average person who ever initiated is computed as the amount the average person using at that age consumes times the probability that a person is using at that age. The probability of someone who ever

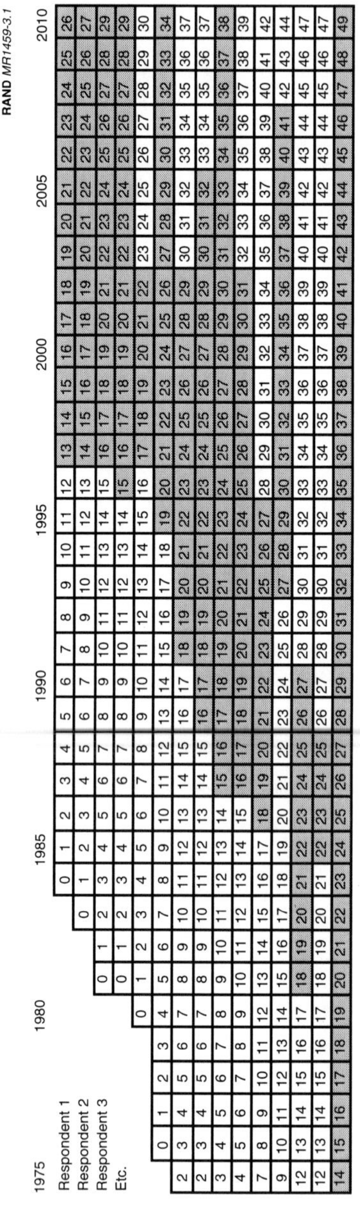

RAND MR1459-3.1

NOTE: Cells denote respondent's age in each year. Shading indicates years in which respondent used drugs.

Figure 3.1—Hypothetical Subset of NHSDA Respondent Drug Use Profiles

uses drugs using drugs at a particular age is, in turn, the product of three probabilities:

1. *The probability of that person using at that particular age if that person is alive and has initiated*

times

2. *The probability of that person having initiated by that particular age given that he or she will initiate at some point*

times

3. *The probability of that person being alive at that age.*

These probabilities may be understood as follows: Given those people from a birth cohort at a given age who have used or will ever use, the third factor in the equation removes the people who have died by that age, the second factor removes those who have not yet initiated, and the first factor removes those who have stopped using. Factor 1 comes from the 1996–1998 NHSDAs (Substance Abuse and Mental Health Services Administration [SAMHSA], 1997, 1998, and 1999a) and is based on past-year prevalence divided by lifetime (i.e., life-to-date) prevalence for respondents.[2] Factor 2 is derived by looking at initiation ages for all NHSDA respondents aged 30 to 34 because the probability of initiating beyond age 30 is very low. (Thus, we can derive this distribution without biasing it by including younger age groups who may have not yet had the opportunity to initiate.) Factor 3 is approximated by the probability of an individual being alive, which is derived from life tables that are available by gender for the overall population and for smokers; we use the tables for the overall population in our alcohol and marijuana calculations and the smokers' tables for our tobacco calculations (Society of Actuaries, 1982).

For each substance, two numbers result from the calculations we just described: predicted lifetime consumption for the average consuming male and predicted lifetime consumption for the average consuming female. We compute an average lifetime consumption esti-

---

[2]For marijuana and tobacco, we compute the probability that someone of X years of age uses the substance, given that the person has initiated. The NHSDA does not report whether someone has initiated *heavy* alcohol use, so we can condition only on whether that person initiated alcohol use at some level.

mate across genders by averaging the male and female consumption estimates, weighting the gender-specific consumption rates with respect to the proportions of male and female users in the NHSDA.

Because Estimation Method 2 is based on a "snapshot" across the NHSDA user population, it ignores cohort effects. That is, use by 30-year-olds in a given survey year may not predict use by 20-year-olds ten years later; differences between the two groups may result instead from the fact that 30-year-olds were born ten years earlier and lived through a different social and drug market regime. Therefore, these estimates may not hold in a year other than the year from which the data are drawn.

Estimation Method 3: Accounting for Evolving Prevalence Patterns Across the Population

Estimation Method 3 is an attempt to account for evolving prevalence patterns across the population. For Estimate 3, we build individual lifetime consumption records. Records of such drug use are, of course, not available from a single NHSDA. Instead, we devised a proxy. We computed lifetime consumption for each user in the NHSDA as the sum of estimated prior use plus estimated future use. Estimated prior use is assumed to be the current level of use times the number of years since initiation.[3] Future use is calculated similarly to the way it is calculated for Estimate 2. It is the sum of the products (for each year from the respondent's current age to age 95) of the following age-specific equation: *the expected level of use given that the respondent is currently a user* times *the probability of the respondent being a user given that the respondent is alive* times *the probability of the respondent being alive*. The first factor, expected use given that one is a user, is calculated differently from the way it is calculated in Estimation Method 2 to account for changing prevalence rates through time.

We next describe the results of applying these three estimation methods to measuring use of marijuana, tobacco, and alcohol.

---

[3]Estimates of age at initiation are, of course, subject to error, but it has been shown that memories of tobacco smoking going back 20 years or more correspond well with reports of smoking made at the time (Bernaards et al., 2001).

Results of Applying the Three Estimation Methods to Marijuana Use

For Estimation Method 1, we sum the estimates of marijuana consumed per year from 1988 through 2000 and divide that sum by the number of initiates during that time (27 million for the entire time period).[4] The Office of National Drug Control Policy (ONDCP, 2000) estimates that the amount of marijuana consumed during that time period was 11,400 metric tons, so our method yields an estimate of 420 grams per lifetime of use, which is equivalent to 1,125 joints (marijuana cigarettes), assuming 0.375 grams per joint. At a price of $300 per ounce, it is also the equivalent of $4,500 in lifetime spending on marijuana per initiate. Since the distribution of consumption patterns is skewed, the median amount spent is presumably substantially less than this, with a smaller number of very heavy users raising the average.

For Estimation Method 2, we compute from the NHSDA the average number of days that marijuana was reported to have been used during the past year for persons of each gender and by age for ages 12 through 95 (see Appendix B for details). After adjusting for the probability someone uses at those ages, given that they ever used, and summing those numbers of days, the resulting estimate is 1,365 self-reported days of marijuana smoking throughout the course of a person's life.

For Estimation Method 3, we compute past-year marijuana consumption per user, just as we did in computing Estimate 2. We then compute future lifetime consumption, as was explained in our general discussion of Estimation Method 3. Averaging over all users, this method yields an estimate of 590 self-reported days of marijuana use in a lifetime, per initiate. The discrepancy between Estimates 2 and 3 is due to the fact that in Estimate 3, prior marijuana use is obtained by multiplying the current-use level by the number of years since initiation of marijuana use. It may not be uncommon for people to consume marijuana heavily for a modest period of time and then to

---

[4]Marijuana initiations for 1988 to 1992 are from Johnson et al. (1996). For 1994 to 1998, data are from SAMHSA (http://www.samhsa.gov/oas/nhsda/PE1996/HTTOC.htm). Numbers for 1993, 1999, and 2000 were unavailable and were imputed using linear interpolation or regression imputation.

subsequently use marijuana more sporadically for a number of years. If so, Estimate 3 mistakenly projects the current, relatively low levels of use back to all prior years, including those that were actually characterized by more-intense use.

We now have estimates expressed in different units of usage: grams in Estimate 1 and NHSDA self-reported days of use in Estimates 2 and 3. To convert all estimates to grams, we observe that between 1996 and 1998, the NHSDA documented 4.3 billion days of self-reported marijuana use, and over the same period the ONDCP (2000) reported total consumption of 2,800 metric tons, suggesting 0.64 grams per day of NHSDA self-reported use. At that "conversion" rate, Estimates 2 and 3 become 880 and 380 grams, respectively.[5] (Conversion to grams in this fashion has the virtue of compensating for the fact that the NHSDA most likely underestimates consumption, because users underreport and because the heaviest users are not household members and thus not included in the survey.)

Results of Applying the Three Estimation Methods to Tobacco Use

We have estimates on the number of cigarette-smoking initiators for each year from 1979 through 1999 and for the number of cigarettes consumed in the United States.[6] The estimated total number of cigarettes consumed from 1975 to 1999 is 13.9 trillion (Centers for Disease Control, 2000), and based on Johnson et al. (1996) and SAMHSA (1996a, 1997, 1998, 1999a, 2000b), we estimate the number of initiates during that time to be 72 million. From these figures, we derive Estimate 1—the total number of cigarettes consumed in a lifetime—to be 193,000, or 9,700 packs in a lifetime, equivalent to a pack-a-day habit lasting 26.5 years.

For Estimates 2 and 3, we identify current smokers as those who have reported smoking during the past month. To compute the number of cigarettes smoked per year, we multiply 12 months by the average number of cigarettes per day smoked in the past month times the av-

---

[5] Conversely, applying the inverse of the conversion factor to the amount by weight in Estimate 1 yields 660 NHSDA self-reported days of use.

[6] The estimate for 1998 was missing and thus was imputed via interpolation.

erage number of days on which cigarettes were smoked during the past month. (For more details, see Appendix B.) Estimate 2 of expected lifetime consumption works out to be 102,000 cigarettes, or about 5,100 packs per lifetime. Estimate 3 is 87,000 cigarettes, or about 4,400 packs per lifetime.

For Estimates 2 and 3, we utilize the NHSDA and hence need to account for underreporting by converting self-reported use into actual estimates of the lifetime consumption of cigarettes. The Centers for Disease Control and Prevention (CDC) reports that 1.45 trillion cigarettes were consumed in the United States in 1996 through 1998. The NHSDA self-reports would suggest that only 810 billion cigarettes were consumed during that same time, which is just 56 percent of the CDC reported total. Thus, to correct for underreporting in the NHSDA, we divide our estimates of the number of self-reported cigarettes used per person in the NHSDA by 0.56 in computing Estimates 2 and 3. The resulting estimates are 183,000 cigarettes, or 9,100 packs, for Estimate 2, and 157,000 cigarettes, or 7,800 packs, for Estimate 3.

Results of Applying the Three Estimation Methods to Alcohol Use

Alcohol initiation data are available going back to 1962 (Johnson et al., 1996). We have alcohol consumption data (National Institute on Alcohol Abuse and Alcoholism [NIAAA], 2001a, 2001b) on the total number of gallons of ethanol consumed in the U.S. for 1970 through 1998, as well as the per capita consumption of alcohol in the United States going back to 1962. Using these two sources, we estimate the total consumption for 1962 through 1969 by linearly extrapolating the number of drinkers, based on the 1970 through 1998 estimates, back to 1962 and multiplying by the per capita consumption numbers.[7] By this method, the total number of persons initiating any alcohol use from 1962 through 1998 was 143 million. The total number

---

[7]The number of persons upon which the per capita figure is based for 1970 through 1998 is derived by dividing the total number of gallons consumed per year by the number of gallons consumed per person. The reference population for 1970 through 1998 is that of persons aged 14 or older, whereas the reference population for prior years is for persons aged 15 or older. We ignore this small discrepancy in our calculations.

of gallons of ethanol consumed was 16.1 billion, yielding an average consumption per user of 113 gallons for Estimate 1.

We are not interested in alcohol use per se, however, because, in contrast to the other substances we discuss here, moderate alcohol use is not regarded as imposing significant net costs on society. We are interested in alcohol abuse as measured, for example, in the NHSDA by the number of days during the past year that the respondent reported getting drunk (for details, see Appendix B). The NHSDA for 1997 reports 1.18 billion self-reported instances of getting drunk in the past year, and NIAAA reports total consumption of 470 million gallons of ethanol in 1997. Furthermore, about 1.57 people try alcohol for every person who ever initiates at least monthly use.[8] Hence, Estimate 1 is calculated as follows: *113 gallons of lifetime ethanol consumption for any type of user* multiplied by *the 1.57 persons who have ever used alcohol for each person who has ever used it monthly,* yielding *177 gallons of ethanol consumed by anyone for every person who has used monthly.* Dividing 1.18 billion self-reported instances of drunkenness by 470 million gallons of ethanol consumed (in 1997) implies 2.5 self-reported instances of drunkenness per gallon of ethanol consumed by anyone. If that number is multiplied by the 177 gallons of ethanol consumed by anyone for every person who has used monthly, the result is 440 lifetime self-reported instances of drunkenness for every person who has used monthly.[9]

Note that while we now have the right *measure* of alcohol use, we can only approximate the right *number.* The right number would be obtained with (1) the ratio of self-reported drunkenness incidents to ethanol consumption that applies only to those who have initiated monthly use and (2) the lifetime ethanol consumption for monthly users. The ratio in the first statement could be larger or smaller than the 2.5 incidents per gallon that apply to all users, and the figure in the second statement could be larger or smaller than 1.57 times the average user's consumption.

---

[8]The 1992 and 1993 NHSDA asked respondents at what age they had first used alcohol monthly.

[9]This calculation followed analogously for calculating the alternate problem-drinking measure—the number of times at least five drinks have been consumed on one occasion.

For Estimates 2 and 3, the annual consumption of alcohol by abusers is estimated from the NHSDA using the same variables. Estimate 2 is 580 self-reported incidents of drunkenness and Estimate 3 is 894 such incidents.

Note that all the alcohol estimates are in terms of self-reported instances of getting drunk. We have no way to correct these estimates for underreporting. However, this does not affect the eventual social-benefit calculations, which are of the form: *dollars saved per participant* equals *instances per participant (Factor 1 x Factor 2)* times *percent reduction of instances (Factor 3 x . . . x Factor 9)* times *social cost per instance (Factor 10)*. Instances are in the numerator and the denominator and thus cancel out; therefore, it does not matter whether we use self-reported or actual instances. If it were possible to substitute the latter, Factor 1 x Factor 2 would increase and, with Factor 10's denominator increasing by the same amount, Factor 10 would decrease in proportion, yielding the same result.

Summary

Table 3.1 contains the three estimates of lifetime consumption obtained for marijuana, tobacco, and alcohol. In Table 3.2, we convert these estimates to low, middle (base), and high estimates by taking the minimum, average, and maximum of these three estimates and rounding to the nearest 25 (or the nearest 100 for cigarettes).[10] Table 3.2 also lists the low, base, and high estimates for cocaine, which were borrowed from Caulkins et al. (1999).

WHAT IS THE PROBABILITY THAT SOMEONE WILL BECOME A USER?

To estimate lifetime consumption per person in a birth cohort from lifetime consumption per initiate, we need to know how many people would initiate use. For all four substances of interest, we compute

---

[10]We round here and in the next section of this chapter because, in attempting to establish reasonable upper and lower bounds, it makes little sense to claim that the upper bound must be, for example, 9,667 packs of cigarettes while 9,700 packs is not reasonable. We hold our middle estimates to a similar degree of precision (or imprecision) as our bounds.

Table 3.1

Summary of Estimated Lifetime Consumption for Marijuana, Tobacco, and Alcohol

Substance	Unit of Consumption	Estimated Lifetime Consumption		
		Estimate 1	Estimate 2	Estimate 3
Marijuana	Grams	422	876	379
Tobacco	Packs of cigarettes	9,667	9,127	7,826
Alcohol	Number of self-reported instances of drunkenness	444	580	894

Table 3.2

Summary of Low, Middle, and High Estimates of Lifetime Consumption

Substance	Unit of Consumption	Estimated Lifetime Consumption		
		Low	Middle	High
Cocaine	Grams	225	350	475
Marijuana	Grams	375	550	875
Tobacco	Packs of cigarettes	7,800	8,900	9,700
Alcohol	Number of self-reported instances of drunkenness	425	650	900

the fraction of people in a cohort who have ever used drugs at all or ever used alcohol monthly at some point in their lives. We cannot, of course, determine that fraction with certainty for current and future cohorts, but looking at past data is informative nonetheless.

Figure 3.2 shows the proportion of people who reported that they have ever used cocaine, marijuana, or tobacco in the 1996 through 1998 NHSDAs and those who have reported ever drinking monthly in the 1992 or 1993 NHSDA.[11, 12] The proportion ever using, also known

---

[11]Because the 1996 through 1998 NHSDA surveys do not contain the heavy-alcohol-use measures of interest, we follow Caulkins et al. (1999) and use the 1992 through 1993 NHSDA data here.

[12]The data shown in Figure 3.2 have been smoothed in two ways. First, we averaged the data for each age shown. Thus, for age 45, we averaged the percentage of 45-year-olds reporting that they had ever used cocaine, marijuana, or tobacco in the 1996,

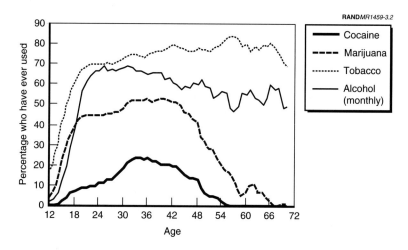

Figure 3.2—Proportions of Various Birth Cohorts Who Report
Substance Use

as "lifetime prevalence," i.e., lifetime-to-date prevalence, varies by age. The proportion is low for people who are young at the time of the survey because they have not yet reached all of the ages during which initiation is commonplace. We would expect rates for the younger cohorts to rise over time as they age. Particularly for cocaine and marijuana, the proportion is low for older cohorts because they have passed through the ages of peak initiation when those drugs were much less available and were less commonly used than they are today. For each substance, we derive, from Figure 3.2, assumed low, middle, and high proportions of a current cohort who would use in the absence of prevention.

1997, and 1998 surveys and computed the average for those reporting they had ever used alcohol monthly in the 1992 and 1993 surveys. Second, these average numbers were then averaged with those of the two immediately adjacent cohorts (i.e., a three-year moving average was calculated). Thus, to derive the percentage shown in the figure for 45-year-olds, the three-survey averages for 44-, 45-, and 46-year-olds were averaged.

Estimating Initiation of Cocaine Use

The proportion who ever used cocaine is low for those who were over 50 in 1996 through 1998 because they had passed through the ages of peak initiation during a time period when cocaine was neither as plentiful nor as popular as it has been in recent years. Just like the low proportions for younger cohorts, this extreme value does not provide the best basis for predicting proportions of future cohorts who will ever use cocaine. It could be argued that we have already seen the worst of cocaine initiation, at least for a while, because the dangers of cocaine use are now widely recognized. The lifetime prevalence of use, as shown in Figure 3.2, peaks at 24 percent (ages 33 through 36), so we take 24 percent as an upper-bound estimate of the proportion of future cohorts who would initiate in the absence of a prevention program.

Initiation rates are far lower now than they were when the cohorts now aged 32 through 36 were young. Indeed, the cocaine epidemic stabilized to a substantial degree in the 1990s. For our conservative estimate of future baseline initiation rates, we imagine a persistence of this relatively stable situation, with no "rebound epidemic." Obviously, this is not literally a lower bound. Theoretically, it is possible that baseline initiation for future cohorts will be zero (in which case, even the best prevention program would avert no cocaine use), but we view persistence of the status quo as a more plausible optimistic scenario.

So, for a low estimate, we work from the fact that, in steady state, if the number of people initiating cocaine use in an average recent year is divided by cohort size, the result is the proportion ever using cocaine. We compute the average cohort size from the NHSDA along with the average number of initiations per year; there were 430,000 cocaine initiations in 1996 (SAMHSA, 2000b); 430,000 in 1997 (SAMHSA, 1999a); and 560,000 in 1998 (SAMHSA, 1998), for an average of 470,000 initiations. With an average cohort size of 3.9 million, which is computed for cohorts aged 13 through 45 in 1997, this computation yields an initiation rate of 12 percent. We take this figure as our lower-bound estimate, 24 percent as our upper estimate, and the average, 18 percent, as our middle estimate.

Estimating Initiation of Marijuana Use

For marijuana, NHSDA self-reported lifetime prevalence of use peaks at 53 percent (age 39), but other sources suggest the true figure is higher. Johnson et al. (1996) report peak lifetime prevalence of self-reported marijuana use of 66 percent in 1987 for 19- through 28-year-olds who were followed up after high school by the Monitoring the Future study (see http://monitoringthefuture.org). Recognizing that some individuals might still initiate after that age, we round the 66 percent figure up to 70 percent as our upper-bound estimate of the proportion of a future cohort who will use marijuana. For a lower estimate, we observe that for cohorts who came of age after marijuana was generally available and who are old enough to have completed most of their initiation, the proportion of the cohort reporting having initiated was never below 40 percent. We scale this 40 percent figure up by the amount of underreporting suggested by our high estimate, making the lower end of the range *40 percent* times *(70 percent* divided by *53 percent)* or *53 percent* (coincidentally, the same as the self-reported peak). The middle estimate is then 61.5 percent.

Estimating Initiation of Tobacco Use

Youthful initiation into smoking, as indicated by measures such as self-reported lifetime prevalence of cigarette smoking for high school seniors (see http://monitoringthefuture.org/data/00data/pr00t4. pdf), fell substantially during the 1980s but stabilized or crept up slightly in the 1990s. Hence, it is likely that future cohorts will not experience higher prevalences of smoking rates than those observed in the past. Thus, it seems reasonable to take as an upper-bound estimate the maximum proportion of a cohort who have ever smoked, which is observed in Figure 3.2 to be about 85 percent (age 56). As a lower bound, we take the proportion for people who were 18 in the early 1990s (about 70 percent), and as a middle estimate, we take 77.5 percent.

Estimating Initiation of Alcohol Use

We want to estimate the proportion of the cohort who would ever use alcohol monthly in the absence of prevention. The curve for lifetime prevalence of monthly alcohol use in Figure 3.2 is relatively flat for ages 20 through 40, and then it decreases for older cohorts. The alcohol curve peaks at 69 percent, so we use that figure as our upper bound. The historical low rate of monthly alcohol use occurs at age 57 (47 percent of the cohort), which we take as our lower bound, with the cohort average (58 percent) as our middle estimate.[13]

Summary

The estimates just given for percentages initiating substance use are summarized in Table 3.3. We anticipate that most persons will try marijuana or tobacco or will drink alcohol monthly at some point in their lives. Cocaine will stay restricted to a minority, although a substantial one.

HOW SHOULD PRESENT AND FUTURE QUANTITIES BE COMPARED? (THE DISCOUNT FACTOR)

It is customary in social policy analyses to recognize that people generally, including policymakers and taxpayers, like to receive their benefits as soon as possible and like to defer costs as long as possible. Customarily, this preference is quantified by applying a constant real discount rate (4 percent per year in this case) to intertemporal trade-offs, and it is important to apply the same rate to both dollars and

Table 3.3

Estimates of the Percentage of a Cohort Who Would Use Substances If Not Exposed to Prevention

Substance	Low Estimate	Middle Estimate	High Estimate
Cocaine	12	18	24
Marijuana	53	61.5	70
Tobacco	70	77.5	85
Alcohol	47	58	69

[13]Proportions of cohorts who ever tried alcohol are much higher than the proportions who report ever using monthly. (If it is true, for example, that 1.57 persons ever use alcohol for every one who initiates monthly use, as we estimated earlier in this chapter, then a guess of the proportion ever using is 1.57 times 58 percent, or 91 percent.)

nonpecuniary benefits and costs. (The reasoning behind this approach is well described by Keeler and Cretin, 1982.) In general, the costs of running a prevention program are all incurred within the first few years. In contrast, the benefits in the form of reduced drug use and the associated social costs accrue over many years, and in the case of alcohol and cigarettes, often for many decades. Hence, this time frame preference for receipt of benefits lowers the effective social benefit per program participant or per dollar invested in prevention compared with what the benefit would be in the absence of "discounting."

The eventual benefits of prevention are in the form of percentage reductions in the drug usage expected without prevention. To the extent possible, we discount that anticipated stream of future consumption so that percentage reductions taken against it will reflect a preference for receiving benefits earlier. In doing so, we derive a ratio of discounted to undiscounted usage that can then be multiplied by the product of Factors 1 and 2 to yield a single present value of expected future use. That ratio is the discount factor, Factor 3. It reflects differences in the lifetime profile of substance use. For substances such as alcohol and tobacco that have longer use profiles, the discount factor would be lower and so would the discounted or present value of future use, relative to the undiscounted value.

The elements of the discount factor are calculated as follows. To obtain undiscounted future use, we add up, over all possible initiation ages, *the probability of initiating at each age* times *expected lifetime consumption for people who initiate at that age.* To put it another way, we take the average of expected lifetime consumption totals across all ages, weighted by the probability of initiating at each age. To obtain discounted future use, we do the same thing, except that we use the *present value* of expected lifetime consumption for people who initiate at each age. [14]

---

[14] At a 4 percent annual discount rate, the present value of a consumption stream in year one is *the consumption in year one,* plus *the consumption in year two* divided by *1.04,* plus *the consumption in year three* divided by *1.04 squared,* plus *the consumption in year four* divided by *1.04 cubed,* plus *the consumption in year five* divided by *1.04 to the fourth power,* and so on. Year one is the year of program implementation, so for initiation ages following that year, some early terms in this series will be zero. We use a 4 percent discount rate because it is typical of the rate used in analyses relating to so-

Not all the values we need, however, are available. In particular, although we know the total future use expected of someone initiating at a given age, we do not know the use pattern by year. We therefore cannot figure out the present value of expected lifetime consumption for each initiation age. We do, however, know the probability that, given any initiation age, a person will still be using at each subsequent age. We therefore take years of use as an approximation to consumption.

Suppose people initiating use at age 20 have a 50 percent probability of using at age 21, a 30 percent probability of using at age 22, a 10 percent probability of using at age 23, and zero thereafter. On average, then, they experience $1.0 + 0.5 + 0.3 + 0.1 + 0.0 = 1.9$ years of use, undiscounted. Discounting at 4 percent annually back to age 12 (the age at which the program is implemented and, hence, costs are incurred), that works out to $0.67 + 0.32 + 0.18 + 0.06 = 1.23$ years of use. The ratio $1.23/1.9 = 0.65$ would then express the relationship between discounted and undiscounted use at that initiation age.[15] This initiation-age-specific discount factor is then multiplied by the total future use expected of someone initiating at that age to yield an estimate of the age-specific present value of expected lifetime consumption. When these steps are done for all initiation ages, the calculation described in the preceding two paragraphs can be carried out and an overall discount factor derived.

We ran through the preceding calculations to obtain an overall discount factor for each drug. The exception was alcohol, for which neither subsequent-use nor persistence data were readily available for various initiation ages. For alcohol, we used the more roughly estimated factor derived by Caulkins et al. (1999, p. 72). That factor was obtained by weighting age-specific NHSDA consumption averages by the U.S. population in each age cohort, finding the present value over the age stream, and then dividing by the undiscounted sum over the age stream.

---

cial welfare, and it is the rate we have used in previous analyses of drug control strategy and thus this rate facilitates comparability.

[15]Of course, we would prefer a factor for average amounts of use; our factor for probabilities of continued use would in general match that factor only if use were constant over the life span. However, we would not expect the difference in eventual results that is caused by this disparity to be substantial.

Chapter Four

SCHOOL-BASED DRUG PREVENTION'S
EFFECTIVENESS AT THE END OF THE PROGRAM

In this chapter, we review and summarize evidence from the literature concerning how much a composite best-practice school-based drug prevention program can be expected to affect early indicators of eventual lifetime use of cocaine, marijuana, tobacco, and alcohol. In particular, we ask how large the prevention effects on each predictor may be at the first follow-up after completion of the program. In Chapter Five, we consider evidence pertaining to the permanence or decay of those effects and relate reduction in the prediction measure to the ultimate reduction in lifetime consumption.

Our goal is not to evaluate a specific prevention program or to compare one prevention program with another. Rather, our goal is to characterize how a hypothetical representative or composite best-practice school-based drug prevention program would affect different types of drug use. We thus combine published effectiveness results for all prevention programs whose evaluations meet certain high standards for quality, as described in the next section.

As we do elsewhere in this book, we give reasonable ranges over which we might expect the effectiveness of a representative model program to vary. The programs chosen, like prevention programs in general, include some that are targeted toward specific substances such as alcohol or tobacco and some with more-generic intent. Some substance-specific programs may do better at reducing use of their target substances or do worse at reducing use of others than our composite results suggest. In the case of substances for which our results are partly based on evaluations of programs specific to those substances, generic programs may not do as well as the composite. To answer the two principal research questions of this study—what is prevention's overall benefit-cost ratio and what is the relative magnitude of the benefits by substance—it is sufficient to derive broadly representative findings.

SELECTION OF PROGRAMS UPON WHICH COMPOSITE ESTIMATES ARE BASED

The literature that addresses drug prevention is large and growing, but it is of uneven quality. For example, of 348 studies of school-based drug prevention in the United States and Canada, only 90 were deemed sufficiently rigorous to be included in Tobler's oft-cited 1993 meta-analysis (Tobler, 1997). Likewise, the Blueprints project of the Center for the Study and Prevention of Violence at the University of Colorado has reviewed more than 450 programs. It found only ten that meet its model-program criteria, which include strong research design and evidence of sustained effect at multiple sites (Elliott, 1997).

Moreover, only a fraction of the high-quality evaluations are relevant to this project. Many are process evaluations that answer questions such as, are teachers, police officers, or peers most effective at delivering drug prevention curricula in a school setting? Other evaluations seek to show that prevention "works" in the sense that it produces a statistically significant impact on some variable thought to be related to drug use, without regard to the magnitude of those impacts or the likely impact on actual drug use.

In our judgment, an evaluation was rigorous if it was published in a peer-reviewed journal and used pre-test/post-test designs with both treatment and control groups, had adequate sample sizes, and had sufficiently long-term follow-up (minimum of two to three years and through ninth grade, and preferably through twelfth grade). The need for follow-up data in high school years limited the list to interventions in the middle school years or later.[1]

---

[1]We thus omit from this analysis results from elementary school interventions such as the Seattle Social Development Project. Such omissions also serve to minimize the effect of variation in performance across grades.

In order for evaluation results to be compatible with our modeling approach, they had to be evaluated in terms of their impact on an entire cohort, not just on certain individuals. Practically speaking, that meant universal programs. (Theoretically, selective or indicated programs could have been included if, for purposes of evaluation, they had been offered to a representative population of participants, not just to those selected, but none meeting the other criteria did so.)

Finally, we can only use studies that provide quantitative estimates of the impact on smoking, drinking, and/or marijuana use; evidence of statistically significant impacts without quantification of the magnitude of those impacts is not enough for present purposes. Likewise, we needed some basis for cost estimation, either direct cost data (which are rare) or a description of the resources used that was sufficiently detailed to enable viable cost estimates to be produced.

We began our search with all studies identified in a recent book (Brounstein and Zweig, 1999) from the Center for Substance Abuse Prevention (CSAP); Drug Strategies' *Safe Schools, Safe Students* report (Drug Strategies, 1994 and 1998); the National Institute on Drug Abuse (NIDA) list of programs that have been studied scientifically (NIDA, 1999); a list of nearly 80 "best practices" prevention programs from CSAP's Center for the Application of Prevention Technology (CAPT); the Blueprint series (Elliott, 1997); a Department of Education review article (Ellickson, 1999); and the more than 100 articles gathered for the study reported by Caulkins et al. (1999). Not surprisingly, there was considerable overlap in the studies identified by these sources. We also sent letters to 11 experts in the prevention field to solicit from them names of other programs satisfying the criteria just listed, including ones that had not been published, and soliciting comments on the programs already identified.

The current study has a broader scope (including programs that measured effects on alcohol or tobacco use alone) than that of Caulkins et al. (1999); for this study, we searched additional sources and further research has been completed in the past few years. For these reasons, results from a greater number of studies are included in this report than were included in the previous study. Specifically, the earlier analysis drew on data from only the Project ALERT and Lifeskills programs. Results from two additional model programs—Midwest Prevention Project (MPP) and Project Northland—are included here in the analysis of the effectiveness of school-based programs at discouraging marijuana use. Three additional model programs—Project TNT (Toward No Tobacco Use), MPP, and Project Northland—are being added to the evaluation of the effectiveness on cigarette smoking initiation, and four additional model programs—Enhanced Alcohol Misuse Prevention Study or "Enhanced AMPS," MPP, Project Northland, and Iowa Strengthening Families—are being added to the evaluation of effectiveness on alcohol initiation. All of these programs are described briefly in Appendix C.

MEASURES OF EFFECTIVENESS

For each of our four drugs of interest, we need a measure of adolescent use that meets two criteria: First, it has to predict, i.e., be correlated with, a long-term consumption measure; second, it has to be directly linked to questions asked in the National Household Survey on Drug Abuse (NHSDA) so that we can quantify the correlation. For marijuana and tobacco, the predictor is initiation of any use—i.e., the probability of someone ever having used the substance. For cocaine, there is not enough adolescent use to support a correlation using an adolescent cocaine use measure, but lifetime cocaine consumption is correlated to the probability of someone ever having used marijuana by a given age, so that probability is our predictor. For alcohol, its use per se is not generally recognized as a problem, and simple consumption of alcohol does not capture the type of problem drinking behavior that prevention programs are typically designed to address. Our long-term measure is thus one of problem use (instances of drunkenness).[2] The probability of someone ever having used alcohol by a given age is not a good predictor of eventual problem use. A better predictor is the probability of that person ever having used alcohol monthly by a certain age. Because program evaluations typically do not ask about initiation into monthly use, we examine *monthly prevalence,* or the probability that an individual has used a drug within the previous month. The association of predictors with lifetime consumption measures is shown in Table 4.1.

---

[2]We also carried through the full set of calculations for an alternate measure of problem use—instances of having consumed at least five drinks on one occasion. The results were of a similar nature (see Chapter Three).

Table 4.1

Predictive (Immediate) Effects of Prevention and Long-Term Consumption

	Cocaine Use	Marijuana Use	Tobacco Smoking	Drunkenness
Initiation of any marijuana use (lifetime prevalence)	X	X		
Initiation of any tobacco use (lifetime prevalence)			X	
Initiation of monthly alcohol use (monthly prevalence)				X

In addition to our direct measures of initiation and monthly prevalence, we report some other measures of annual, monthly, and weekly use. Because data on the direct measures are limited, we use data on prevention's impact on other measures to help establish ranges of likely impacts on our direct measures. We refer to these other measures as "indirect measures."

We focus on differences in these measures between control and treatment groups at program completion; all programs included in our analysis randomized study participants for enrollment in treatment and control groups at baseline. The end of the program is defined as the completion of all regular and booster sessions regardless of grade. This approach is preferable to focusing on effects in a particular grade because the timing and duration of interventions vary across programs—e.g., focusing on effects in the ninth grade may penalize a program that operates in the seventh grade relative to one that operates in the eighth or ninth grades because the effects of the seventh grade program may have decayed by the later grades. (We do account for decay of initial effect, but we do not want to miss periods of effectiveness by measuring initial effect after decay has begun.)

In some cases, the programs fielded an immediate post-program evaluation. In other cases, the evaluation was conducted within a year of completion of the programs. As long as the follow-up evaluation was completed within a year of the termination of the program,

the results are included in our evaluation of short-term program effectiveness.[3] The one exception to this rule is the inclusion of results
from the Lifeskills program. Our review of the literature identified
published quantitative results for Lifeskills only from the twelfth
grade follow-up, three years after the last booster session in ninth
grade. Although no immediate post-program evaluation was published with the sort of data we need, a significant difference in measures of substance use between treatment and control groups
remained in the twelfth grade. We therefore chose to include the
findings of this study in our evaluation of program effectiveness even
though we have no immediate post-program evaluation. This is
consistent with methodology employed in the earlier study.[4]

INDIVIDUAL PROGRAM EFFECTS

The findings concerning prevention's effectiveness at reducing marijuana, tobacco, and alcohol use are presented in Tables 4.2, 4.3, and
4.4, respectively. These tables concisely summarize what the literature reports about middle-school-based drug prevention programs'
effects on drug use in a general population at first follow-up data
collection (based only on information from rigorous evaluations).

In each table, we list the affected drug use measures in order of decreasing term of effect: *Lifetime prevalence,* listed first, is the percentage having initiated any use of the drug—that is, having ever
used the drug. *Annual prevalence* is the percentage having used the
drug within the past year. Monthly, weekly, and (for tobacco) daily
use measures follow. The percentages given are percentage reductions in the usage rates. For example, if 15 percent of the group par-

---

[3]Additional follow-up evaluations that were conducted after the school-based program was completed (e.g., Project ALERT follow-ups) are discussed in Chapter Five
where we estimate the permanence or decay of program effects.

[4]Another reason for including Lifeskills in our calculation of program effectiveness instead of program decay is the fact that we cannot calculate decay without knowledge
of the immediate post-program results from the ninth grade. The published effects for
the twelfth grade confound the results from program effectiveness with those of decay.
Note that if the Lifeskills program's effects decayed over time, then including the
twelfth-grade results alongside results from other programs taken sooner after completion provides a conservative estimate of Lifeskills' effect.

Table 4.2

Prevention's Impact on Marijuana Use: Percentage Difference Between Program Recipients and Controls for Various Indicators at First Available Follow-Up Data Collection

	Project ALERT	Lifeskills	MPP	Project Northland
Lifetime prevalence	–4.9%	—	—	—
Annual prevalence	—	—	—	–14.0%
Monthly use[a]	–5.8%	—	—	—
Monthly prevalence	–20.3%	–7.1%	–26.0%	—
Weekly use	–18.0%	–33.3%	–22.8%	—

[a]Project ALERT constructs a measure of regular monthly use of each substance from responses to the number of times within a year that the individual reported using the substance. If the response rates were greater than 12, then the respondent was considered to be a regular monthly user. This is different from the other programs that reported estimates for only past-month prevalence (listed as "Monthly prevalence" in the table).

Table 4.3

Prevention's Impact on Tobacco Use: Percentage Difference Between Program Recipients and Controls for Various Indicators at First Available Follow-Up Data Collection

	Project ALERT	Project Northland	Project TNT[a]	Lifeskills	MPP
Lifetime Prevalence	–4.3%	–19.2%	–21.5%	—	—
Monthly use	–0.7%	—	—	—	—
Monthly prevalence	–2.0%	—	—	–19.7%	–31.5%
Weekly use	–7.9%	—	–64.3%	–18.5%	–30.3%
Daily use/ pack of cigarettes a day	–1.6%	—	—	–20.8%	—

[a]Numbers shown for Project TNT represent those for the combined model intervention.

Table 4.4

**Prevention's Impact on Alcohol Use: Percentage Difference Between
Program Recipients and Controls for Various Indicators at First Available
Follow-Up Data Collection**

	Project ALERT	Iowa	Lifeskills	MPP	Project Northland	Enhanced AMPS
Lifetime prevalence	–4.1%	–26.0%	—	—	—	—
Annual prevalence	—	—	—	—	—	–3.3%
Monthly use	–5.4%	—	—	—	—	—
Monthly prevalence	–2.1%	—	–1.7%	–30.8%	–19.2%	—
Weekly use	+2.2%	—	–8.6%	–42.0%	–29.1%	—
Heavy drinking	—	–24.4%	–16.3%	—	—	–4.5%

ticipating in a particular prevention program initiated marijuana use, and 20 percent of the control group did so, the result is a 25 percent difference and would be listed in the lifetime prevalence row of Table 4.2 as –25%.[5] The tables include results reported as being not statistically significant by the original evaluations as well as those that were.[6]

A quick look at Tables 4.2 through 4.4 reveals important insights regarding the difficulty of trying to evaluate the overall effectiveness of prevention at discouraging substance use in general.

- First, as we have already suggested, there is a great deal of heterogeneity in the number and types of substances that are evaluated across various programs. Some programs, such as Project TNT, Enhanced AMPS, and Iowa Strengthening Families, are specialized and target the use and/or initiation of just one substance. Other programs are much broader in scope and develop

---

[5]Formally, for each program at time t, we calculate the program's effect as $(C_t - T_t)/C_t$, where C_t represents the prevalence measure for the control group at time t and T_t represents the prevalence measure for the treatment group at time t.

[6]Some studies (including Iowa Strengthening Families) reported treatment/control differences at first follow-up that were statistically significant in raw form but not significant after controls for demographic characteristics and attrition were accounted for. The numbers reported in the tables control for these factors.

curriculum (and evaluations) targeting the use and/or initiation of multiple substances.

- Second, even when results are reported for the same drug and the same measure, the magnitude of the effects can vary widely across programs. For example, MPP reduced monthly prevalence of marijuana use by 26 percent. Project ALERT also managed a reduction of more than 20 percent. But another sound program, Lifeskills, managed only a 7 percent reduction. Such variations introduce substantial uncertainty into the inference of a composite result.

- A third issue is the heterogeneity in the indicators of use that are examined across programs that evaluate the same substances. For example, Project Northland evaluated only the annual prevalence of marijuana use while Project ALERT, Lifeskills, and MPP considered measures of monthly and weekly use of marijuana. Even within the same type of indicator (e.g., heavy use) there is variation in how that indicator is constructed across studies. For example, Lifeskills has two different measures of heavy drinking, one that evaluates the number of instances when three or more drinks were consumed on a single drinking occasion and a dichotomous variable indicating if the individual reported being drunk at least once in the past month. The Iowa Strengthening Families program defines heavy drinking as having ever been drunk. Enhanced AMPS defines heavy drinking as a ten-variable index of alcohol misuse. Although measured differently across programs, heavy drinking is reported as a single-use category in the tables for ease of exposition and because the numbers will ultimately be aggregated.

- A fourth issue is the construction of the control and treatment groups across programs. Some programs (Lifeskills, MPP) do not differentiate between pre-program nonusers and users whereas other programs (Project ALERT, Enhanced AMPS) break out both treatment and control groups into pre-program nonusers, experimenters, and users. Program effects are then reported for each subgroup. In order to obtain a single measure of program effectiveness for these programs that is comparable to those from other programs, we aggregated findings across these different treatment and control groups. Appendix D illustrates how this was done in the case of marijuana use indicators for Project

ALERT. Similar calculations were used to collapse findings across three different baseline types of drinkers in the Enhanced AMPS project.

AGGREGATE PROGRAM EFFECTS

Our next task is to aggregate the information in Tables 4.2 through 4.4 into performance parameters describing the effectiveness of a hypothetical composite or representative "best practices" prevention program. There is no one definitive or "right" way to do this aggregation, so we use four alternative methods. Each of these methods generates a different set of high, middle, and low estimates for each drug and use category. In Appendix D, we describe the methods, their results, and the approach we take to aggregating those results into a single set of numbers for each drug and use category.[7] That single set of numbers is shown in Table 4.5.

As can be seen from Table 4.5, we aggregate use into two categories: lifetime prevalence and past-month prevalence. The results given in the table show that the percentage-use reductions associated with prevention programs do not vary consistently across substances.

Table 4.5

Final Estimates of Program Effectiveness

Substance	Measure of Use	Low Estimate	Middle Estimate	High Estimate
Marijuana	Lifetime prevalence	–4.9%	–10.9%	–14.0%
Tobacco	Lifetime prevalence	–4.3%	–16.8%	–21.5%
Alcohol	Past-month prevalence	–1.7%	–12.8%	–30.8%

[7]None of the methods weighs the results from the three programs targeted at single substances (the Iowa, Enhanced AMPS, and TNT programs) differently from the results of the generic programs. Not surprisingly, including the targeted programs raises somewhat the aggregate effectiveness numbers against alcohol and tobacco. We include results from both types of programs because we are interested in a broadly representative model program. Readers who disagree with this approach will regard our results for alcohol and cigarettes as somewhat optimistic, relative to those for alcohol and cocaine.

Depending on whether one is looking at low, middle, or high estimates, or at lifetime or past-month prevalence, any of the three substances may be first or last in percentage reduction. As already indicated, we will be emphasizing the middle estimates of the lifetime measures for marijuana and tobacco and the past-month measure for alcohol. That approach would indicate that prevention's greatest effect is on tobacco and its weakest effect is on marijuana. However, these are only end-of-program effects. They do not take into account what happens to the predictive measures after the program ends, and they do not take into account the implications of the predictive measures for lifetime consumption. Chapter Five delves into these topics.

SCHOOL-BASED PREVENTION'S EFFECTIVENESS AT REDUCING LIFETIME DRUG USE

In Chapter Four, we estimated the effects of school-based prevention on adolescent use of marijuana, alcohol, and tobacco as of the end of the first evaluation follow-up, which we envision as happening in eighth grade in our hypothetical model program. Unfortunately, with only one possible exception among the programs we studied (the Lifeskills program), observed differences between treatment and control groups had disappeared by the end of high school.

At some point, the delay in drug use caused by prevention comes to an end. However, this does not render moot the question of effect on lifetime consumption. Not only is consumption reduced during middle and high school, but there is reason to believe that people who use drugs less extensively as youths will also use drugs less extensively as adults, even if they have tried drugs before leaving high school (Everingham and Rydell, 1994; Kandel and Yamaguchi, 1993; Kandel, 1975). Still, it is important to account quantitatively for this decay in observed effects and delay of initiation. The reason it is important to account for decay and delay is that (as shown later in this chapter) we estimate, for each drug, age-specific initiation rates, with and without prevention, and associate those rates (through National Household Survey on Drug Abuse [NHSDA] data) with percentage changes in lifetime consumption. Decay of the initiation effect thus impinges on estimated lifetime consumption.

It is important throughout this chapter to distinguish between effects on the predictor variables, which we discuss in the first two sections, and effects on lifetime consumption, which we discuss in the last section. The final calculation in this chapter divides the percentage differences in lifetime consumption by the estimates of program effectiveness (shown in Table 4.5) to arrive at Factor 5, the percentage reduction in lifetime consumption for each percentage-point reduction in prevalence at the end of the program.

MEASURING DECAY OF SHORT-TERM EFFECT

As we have noted, there is extensive literature evaluating prevention programs, but only a small subset of those studies reports quantitative effects based on rigorous evaluations. Fewer still empirically address the permanence of observed program effects. In particular, there is very little information concerning the rate at which the program effects decay after the program, including the booster sessions, ends. There is something approaching a consensus that decay does not begin until after the end of booster sessions. And with one conspicuous exception, the studies with published long-term evaluations find that program effects are gone within four or five years after the program is completed, typically around the senior year in high school (e.g., Peterson et al., 2000; Ellickson, Bell, and McGuigan, 1993; Flay et al., 1989). However, there is precious little information concerning precisely how this decay occurs. Do effects decay linearly over time? Do they decay faster initially and then approach zero asymptotically? Or does decay follow some other pattern altogether? We simply do not know with any certainty, but in this chapter we review and synthesize what meager information is available.

Most of the programs we examined in Chapter Four published data for only one follow-up past the end of the program, so they provide no information concerning decay. The exception is Project ALERT (two follow-ups separated by three years for each of three drugs).

Given this paucity of information, we decided to consider information from other programs that published long-term follow-up data for at least two years based on a strong but perhaps less than ideal evaluation. Casting this broader net captured several additional studies, but most merely present data from the last follow-up that was conducted and by then the effects have generally disappeared. For example, the Waterloo Smoking Prevention Project published only twelfth-grade results despite having collected five years of post-program data (Flay et al., 1989). Those results show complete decay by the twelfth grade but provide no insight as to the rate of decay leading up to the twelfth grade. Similarly, the Hutchinson Smoking Prevention Project (Peterson et al., 2000), which was implemented on third-graders who were followed up for two years post high school, published results only for the twelfth grade and two years post high school, both of which show complete decay of the program effects.

Two exceptions are the Tobacco and Alcohol Prevention Program, or TAPP (Hanson, Malotte, and Fielding, 1988) and the Minnesota Smoking Program (Murray et al., 1987, 1988, and 1989). The TAPP data, however, are not very useful because none of the program effects were significant in any of the follow-ups. The Minnesota Smoking Program is the single best source of information concerning how program effects decay over time because it reports results annually for up to six years and for multiple measures. Unfortunately, there are quite a number of complications in using these results (see Appendix E for more details).

Before proceeding, special note needs to be made of the Lifeskills data. Lifeskills evaluations are the single greatest source—indeed, perhaps the single rigorous source—of evidence that decay in effects may not, or at least need not, be substantially complete by the twelfth grade. In particular, Lifeskills data suggest substantial effects remain in the twelfth grade, but we cannot use those data directly to estimate decay between the end of the program in the ninth grade and the twelfth grade because the ninth-grade Lifeskills data are not published in a form that allows comparison with the twelfth-grade results.[1] The ninth- and twelfth-grade data are comparable for the program's "high-fidelity" subsample, but we have reservations about following the Lifeskills evaluation in separating a high-fidelity subsample from the rest of the treatment group.[2]

---

[1]Repeated efforts to obtain year-by-year outcome data from Lifeskills failed.

[2]Only a subset (the "high-fidelity" subset) of schools in the treatment group was able to fully implement the Lifeskills program. Results for this group relative to controls might indicate how effective the program is when fully implemented. However, if there are unobserved school-level factors that drive both the ability to implement a program and the prevalence of delinquent behavior, it might give a very biased indication of program effects—e.g., if chaotic schools both promote drug use and undermine rigorous implementation of special curricula, focusing on the high-fidelity schools might not represent the effectiveness of the program if it is universally implemented,

We infer from the evaluations cited in Chapter Four two qualitative descriptions of program effects over time. Decay of prevention's effect on the short-term predictor does not begin until after the program, including booster sessions, terminates and, as discussed in the beginning of this chapter, by the twelfth grade the effect has decayed to zero. Because of the evidence concerning the importance and success of booster sessions, we envision a model program as having such sessions. So, if a model intervention begins with 12-year-olds (sixth-graders), we suppose that booster sessions, and hence full effectiveness, persist through age 14 (eighth grade). That is, whatever program effectiveness we estimate based on the evaluations presented in Chapter Four, we assume it applies without decay from ages 12 through 14. We presume that decay is complete by age 18, so the remaining question is how large the effects are at ages 15, 16, and 17 (i.e., grades 9, 10, and 11) as a percentage of the effects for ages 12 through 14.[3, 4]

There is no reason a priori to assume that the decay curves are identical for each drug, and what little evidence we have suggests differences across the drugs. We thus seek to fill in the effect sizes for ages 15, 16, and 17 separately for alcohol, tobacco, and marijuana. Using different assumptions, we estimate two decay curves for each drug. However, because the decay curves for each drug are drawn from separate interventions, and differences in decay across programs may exceed differences in decay rates across substances, we also estimate a generic decay curve that we can apply to all drugs equally. We therefore have three decay options—the two specific ones and the generic one—for each substance. To proceed with our "best guess" estimate of Factor 5, we choose the curve yielding the intermediate overall effectiveness for each substance. That curve for each substance, which we term the "primary decay" model, is one of the

---

as we assume for our model program. Hence, we rely only on data comparing the full treatment group to the corresponding controls.

[3]There is no perfect mapping between age and grade—e.g., not all 15-year-olds are in the ninth grade, and not all ninth-graders are 15. Nevertheless, we adopt this simplification here because it is more convenient to discuss implementation times and decay in terms of grades; however, the NHSDA reports key quantities by age.

[4]We do not presume that the effects are necessarily smaller in grade 9 than they are in grade 8. That is, although we use the term "decay" because over the long-run effects dissipate, the "decay" can be zero or even negative in the short run.

substance-specific curves. To generate low and high estimates of Factor 5, we use the decay curves generating lower and higher overall effectiveness.

The decay functions we use are shown in Figure 5.1. For information on all the curves and further details on our methods for estimating decay curves, see Appendix E.

TAKING ACCOUNT OF LENGTH OF INITIATION DELAY

The question of initiation delay is not necessarily completely addressed by specifying fully the decay curve for observed effect size, as we have just done. If effects on lifetime prevalence, i.e., life-to-date prevalence, have fully decayed by age 18, then the proportions of treatment and control group members who have initiated by age 18 are the same. That is, cumulative initiation through age 18, or equivalently, the sum of initiation by year through age 18, is the same for each group.

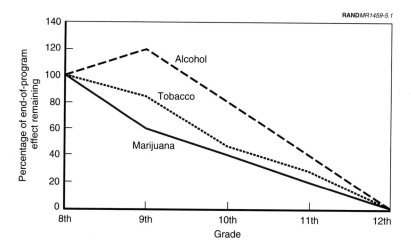

Figure 5.1—Best-Guess Decay Functions Assumed for End-of-Program Effects on Initiation

This pattern is shown in Figure 5.2 for marijuana: Relative initiation to date decreases from ages 12 to 14, then the decrement wears off. This pattern implies that if prevention suppresses initiation in the early years (e.g., ages 12 to 14) then necessarily initiation rates are actually *higher* in the treatment groups in some other years leading up to age 18 (i.e., ages 16 and 17; see Figure 5.3). That is, initiation is deferred from middle school to high school, so initiates among the high-school-age prevention participants include not only those who would have initiated in high school without the program but also the deferred middle-school initiates. Given this annual initiation profile, there is little reason to presume that the treatment group's initiation rates would be suppressed in subsequent years relative to those of nonparticipants. We call this view the "conservative scenario" view of initiation delay and we used it in calculating our baseline esti-

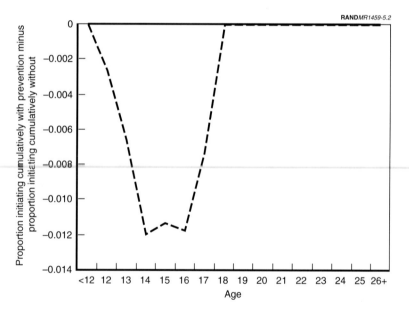

Figure 5.2—Initiation of Marijuana Use with Prevention as a Decrement
from Initiation Without Prevention, Life to Date, Best-Guess End-of-
Program Effectiveness, Linear Decay

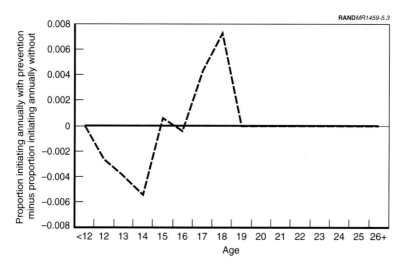

Figure 5.3—Initiation of Marijuana Use with Prevention as a Decrement
from Initiation Without Prevention, Annually, Best-Guess End-of-Program
Effectiveness, Linear Decay

mates in Table 2.2 and elsewhere. For example, our summary conclusion (see Chapter Two) that prevention's drug-related benefits are
worth about $840 (versus a cost of about $150) is predicated on this
conservative view of no impact on initiation rates for ages 19 or
higher.

But the decay of some predictive measures leaves open the possibility for a longer delay of initiation. Suppose the prevention measure in
question was past-year initiation. Then decay to zero by age 18
would imply that initiation in the treatment group was lower for a
period of time (e.g., at ages 12 to 14) and equal by age 18, but not
necessarily ever higher than in the control group. Thus, at age 18,
cumulative initiation would be lower in the treatment group than in
the control group, and those "deferred initiates" must initiate after
age 18, if at all.

Is there any evidence that what decays by age 18 is current, not lifetime, initiation? Perhaps there is. The measures that the literature
reports as decaying by age 18 (including but not limited to studies

contributing to our estimates in Chapter Four) rarely include past-year initiation and some are in fact direct measures of lifetime prevalence, but others pertain to measures of recent use (e.g., past-year or past-month use). Because most people who try illicit drugs use only briefly, the measures of recent use and past-year initiation for youths often move in tandem. So, decay in effects on recent use could be indicative of decay in past-year initiation. In light of this and the Lifeskills evaluation results discussed in Chapter Four, the assumption that prevention has no effect on initiation beyond age 18 may be too conservative.

If, however, the conservative scenario were wrong, there would remain the question of what happens to those individuals who would have initiated by age 18 but did not do so because of the prevention program. At one extreme, they might initiate the day after graduation. Or they might never initiate. There is literally no way to know for sure what happens to these individuals after the final follow-up data collection because, by definition, we do not have data on their behavior.

In our analyses, we carry through the calculations under two other scenarios in addition to the conservative scenario. In these second and third scenarios, it is only differences in past-year initiation that are presumed to have decayed by age 18. In the second scenario, which we term the "optimistic scenario," the cumulative difference in initiation between treatment and control groups is expected to disappear soon thereafter. In particular, it is spread over ages 19 through 21 in proportion to baseline initiation at those ages (see Figure 5.4). The result is that cumulative initiation by age 21 is the same for treatment and control groups (see Figure 5.5). Note that because it is the past-year initiation effect that is decaying (ages 14 to 18; see Figure 5.4), the lifetime reduction relative to no prevention is still accumulating through the high school years, beyond what is assumed in the conservative scenario (see Figure 5.5).

In the third scenario, which we term the "very optimistic scenario," those whom prevention has deterred from initiating by age 18 are presumed to subsequently initiate at the same rate as individuals who historically have not initiated by age 18. As shown in Figure 5.4,

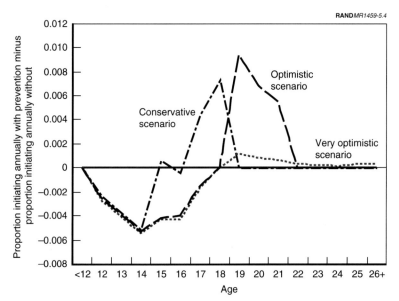

NOTE: Values for nearly superimposed curves are identical; slight offset is for readability.

Figure 5.4—Marijuana Initiation Scenarios, Viewed Annually, Best-Guess End-of-Program Effectiveness, Linear Decay

this scenario shares with the optimistic scenario the notion that it is the annual initiation effect that is decaying by age 18, but the compensatory increment relative to no prevention is flattened here and largely eliminated. Historically, about 23 percent of individuals who have not initiated marijuana use by age 18 do subsequently initiate, most within three years and a few later on in life. In this third scenario, then, someone whom prevention has deterred from initiating marijuana use by age 18 is modeled as having only a 23 percent chance of ever using marijuana (with most of that risk being in the next three years). Thus, 23 percent of those who do not initiate because of prevention eventually do initiate, while the other 77 percent

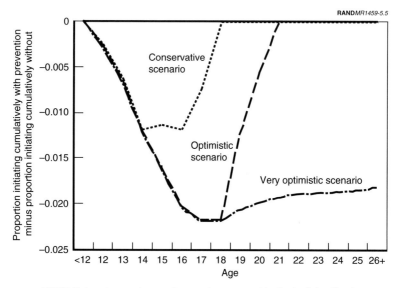

NOTE: Values for nearly superimposed curves are identical; slight offset is for readability.

Figure 5.5—Marijuana Initiation Scenarios, Viewed Cumulatively, Best-Guess End-of-Program Effectiveness, Linear Decay

never do.[5] (The accumulated decrement in Figure 5.5 stays at 77 percent of its peak.)

The second scenario is only modestly more optimistic than the first. The third scenario is substantially more bullish about the permanence of prevention's effects. We choose the terms "optimistic" and "very optimistic" (rather than, say, "medium" and "optimistic") because in contrast to the short-term effect sizes calculated in Chapter

---

[5]The best data we have on decay rates are for tobacco use and, as they pertain to recent use, the data are consistent with any of these initiation delay scenarios. The ALERT (marijuana) and Iowa (alcohol) decay data are for lifetime prevalence and so are most consistent with the conservative delay scenario. However, those data are from just one program each. That the programs apparently did not affect initiation beyond age 18 does not necessarily mean that no program could, so it is not unreasonable to examine more-optimistic delay scenarios.

Four, we think of the conservative (first) scenario as the baseline scenario. We offer two variants on the more optimistic side simply because for those inclined to be more optimistic it is not obvious a priori how much more optimistic to be. On the other hand, we believe there is no reason to consider scenarios any more pessimistic than those that project the differences in cumulative initiation to have fully decayed by age 18. (For example, we believe there is no reason to consider "boomerang" scenarios in which model prevention programs that reduce initiation at ages 12 to 14 trigger higher cumulative rates of initiation after age 18.)

We use the conservative scenario for our "best guess" estimates of benefits for all three substances. An argument could be made that a more optimistic scenario for tobacco would be appropriate because the decay data presented earlier characterize current use, not lifetime prevalence. We account for the possibility that this argument is correct in the sensitivity analysis reported in Chapter Two but adhere to the conservative scenario here for two reasons: First, it makes it easier to draw comparisons across substances because they are all treated equally on this dimension. Second, it is conservative with respect to our findings (see Chapter Two) that prevention is likely cost-justified, reductions in tobacco use are the greatest source of social benefits, and reduced marijuana use is only a minor source of benefits. If a more optimistic scenario were appropriate for tobacco, then all of these conclusions would hold with even greater force.

Figure 5.6 repeats the estimates of use shown in Figure 5.5 but in actual values instead of for prevention alone relative to no prevention. As in the previous figures, linear decay and "best guess" end-of-program effectiveness (at 10.9 percent) are assumed. In all scenarios, initiation is depressed relative to a no-prevention baseline for ages 12 through 14, during which time prevention's initial effect is felt. In the conservative scenario, initiation is as high or higher than the no-prevention baseline for ages 15 through 18, so that cumulative initiation through age 18 is unchanged, along with initiation at all subsequent ages. In the other two scenarios, initiation is depressed for ages 15 through 17 as well as for ages 12 through 14. In the "optimistic" scenario, those reductions are "made up" by higher initiation when delays end at ages 19 through 21. In the "very optimistic" scenario, those people whose initiation was delayed past

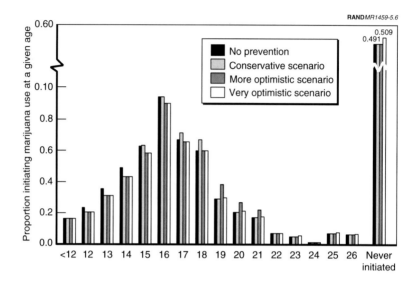

Figure 5.6—Implications of Permanence Assumptions for Age-Specific
Initiation of Marijuana Use, Assuming 10.9 Percent Short-Term Prevention
Effectiveness and Linear Decay of Effect

age 18 are scattered across all the bars to the right of the age-18 bar in
Figure 5.6, including the "Never initiated" bar.

TRANSLATING EFFECTIVENESS PREDICTORS TO RESULTS

Given our estimates of the short-term effectiveness of school-based
prevention programs and decay of those effects, we now wish to
project the associated percentage reduction in lifetime consumption.
For three of the four substances of interest (alcohol, marijuana, and
tobacco), we project this reduction in use on the basis of prevention's short-term effectiveness at reducing a predictive measure for
the same substance. For example, we estimate reductions in lifetime
tobacco use associated with reductions and delays in initiation of
smoking observed through high school. In the case of lifetime cocaine use, however, we use reductions and delays in initiation of
marijuana use as the predictive risk factor because prevention eval-

uations do not measure effects on cocaine use itself in secondary school.

Our Approach

Our method is best understood by examining Table 5.1, which illustrates the calculations for impact on cocaine use, the most complicated case. We know the baseline (no prevention) distribution of ages of marijuana use initiation (the predictive factor in this case) from historical data, specifically from the 1997–1998 NHSDA. The baseline distribution of ages of initiation is drawn from the experience of respondents between the ages of 30 and 34. These individuals are old enough that most of them who will ever initiate have already done so, but they are young enough that they have passed through the ages of peak initiation in relatively contemporary times.

We use the information on prevention's short-term effectiveness (see Chapter Four), decay curve, and initiation delay model (discussed earlier in this chapter) to calculate the corresponding distribution of initiation ages with prevention (see column 2b of Table 5.1). Naturally, the percentage reduction in initiation at each age depends on the effectiveness, decay, and delay assumptions. Thus, Table 5.1 shows the distribution of ages of initiation for just one set of prevention assumptions. In particular, it reflects a "best guess" of effectiveness (10.9 percent reduction in marijuana initiation), the primary or linear model of decay (shown in Figure 5.1), and the "optimistic" view of initiation delay. Thus, the proportion initiating marijuana use at age 12 with prevention (0.0211) is 11 percent lower than the proportion initiating use at age 12 without prevention (0.0237), as determined from NHSDA participants. Age 14 is the last year of 11-percent effectiveness. After that, the effectiveness percentage decays linearly to zero by age 18. By this point, the sum of the differences in initiation has reached 0.0218.[6] In other words, 2.18 percent of the population has had its marijuana use initiation delayed beyond age 18. Under the "optimistic" scenario, that 2.18 percent will initiate in

---

[6]Technically, the age-specific differences cannot simply be summed, because simple summing ignores the population removed from each successive age group by death. But mortality rates are very low at these ages, so we do not account for them.

Table 5.1
Lifetime Cocaine Use by Age of Marijuana Initiation

1 Age of Marijuana Initiation	2 Proportion of Cohort Starting Marijuana Use		3 Proportion of Marijuana Initiates Reporting Ever Having Used Cocaine	4 Mean Number of Self-Reported Days of Cocaine Use by Marijuana Initiates, Undiscounted	5 Discount Factor	6 Mean Number of Self-Reported Days of Cocaine Use by Marijuana Initiates, Discounted
	2a No Prevention	2b With Prevention				
11 or younger	0.0168	0.0168	0.5216	169.1	0.591	99.9
12	0.0237	0.0211	0.5171	137.2	0.593	81.3
13	0.0357	0.0318	0.4995	101.2	0.568	57.5
14	0.0496	0.0442	0.4435	102.4	0.557	57.0
15	0.0634	0.0592	0.3994	75.2	0.539	40.6
16	0.0949	0.0907	0.3523	70.7	0.522	36.9
17	0.0675	0.0660	0.2838	63.8	0.493	31.4
18	0.0602	0.0602	0.2817	65.2	0.478	31.2
19	0.0294	0.0388	0.2319	72.9	0.466	33.9
20	0.0211	0.0278	0.2078	95.0	0.427	40.6
21	0.0172	0.0228	0.2090	80.0	0.410	32.8
22	0.0073	0.0073	0.1786	51.7	0.402	20.8
23	0.0054	0.0054	0.1483	96.1	0.376	36.1
24	0.0019	0.0019	0.1835	61.9	0.369	22.9
25	0.0078	0.0078	0.2020	133.3	0.354	47.2
26 or older	0.0074	0.0074	0.1491	58.1	0.332	19.3
Never used marijuana	0.4907	0.4907	0.0037	87.3	0.505	44.1

the next three years. The 0.0218 difference is spread over the three years in proportion to the baseline initiation numbers (0.0294, 0.0211, and 0.0172). Under this scenario, prevention has no effect on subsequent age-specific marijuana initiation rates or on the percentage who never initiate.[7]

Columns 3 through 6 in Table 5.1 translate the reductions in marijuana initiation into reductions in lifetime cocaine consumption. Column 3 shows, by age of marijuana initiation, the proportion of persons who said they used cocaine at some point. For example, the second row indicates that 51.7 percent of people who started marijuana use at age 12 tried cocaine at some point in their lives. For any drug other than cocaine, the numbers in this column (except in the bottom row of the table) would all be 1 because the short-term and lifetime effects are for the same substance, and everyone who initiates at a given age uses the drug.

Column 4 of Table 5.1, also from the NHSDA, gives the self-reported lifetime days of cocaine use by persons who reported ever using cocaine, for each age of marijuana initiation.[8] Cocaine users who reported starting marijuana use at age 12 reported using cocaine on an average of 137 days over their lives. Because cocaine users make up 52 percent of those initiating marijuana use at age 12, the average number of self-reported days of cocaine use by a person initiating marijuana use at age 12 is 52 percent of 137 or approximately 71 days.

In Chapter Three, we explained the calculation of age-specific discount factors. When that calculation is performed with respect to cocaine use by persons initiating marijuana use at age 12, a discount

---

[7]Under the very optimistic scenario, the 0.0218 difference is spread out proportionally over all rows below the "Age of Marijuana Initiation—18" row in Table 5.1, including the "Never used marijuana" row. In the conservative scenario, delayed initiation begins at age 15, so that the reductions in initiation up to that point are offset by increased initiation between ages 15 and 18. In that scenario, columns 2a and 2b are identical after age 18. (For a graphical view of this scenario, see Figure 5.2.)

[8]Because the data in columns 3 and 4 are empirically derived, the numbers in those columns do not exhibit a smooth decrease with age after early peaks. Number of self-reported days of use shows a peak at age 20 and both self-reported days of use and initiation exhibit an upswing at age 25. These may be random variation or cohort effects. We have no basis for attempting to control for them and simply use them as they are.

factor of 0.593 is obtained. Multiplying that discount factor by 137 days of expected cocaine use produces a present value of 81 days of lifetime use. The 81 days is the discounted self-reported lifetime consumption by those who initiate marijuana use at age 12 *and* initiate cocaine use at some point. Therefore, the average self-reported cocaine use by *any* person initiating marijuana use at age 12 is 42 days in terms of present discounted value (71 days times 0.59, or 81 days times 0.52).

Technically, the information in columns 3 through 6 pertains to self-reported substance use. One would certainly expect substantial underreporting, particularly for cocaine, both because of outright deceit and because heavy users disproportionately fall out of the survey's sample frame. This is a concern, but not a major one, because we are only interested in calculating percentage reductions in use, not absolute quantities. That is, in this chapter, we calculate the percentage reduction in observable, specifically self-reported, use and make the implicit assumption that the percentage reduction in unobserved use is similar. We do not assume that observable use is all use (or even necessarily a large portion of all use).

Given the data in Table 5.1, we can calculate quantities pertaining to an average person over his or her lifetime by taking a weighted sum of the quantities in a column, weighting by the proportion of the population in each row (as expressed in column 2a or 2b). For example, if we are interested in initiation of cocaine use, which is represented by column 3, we weight the numbers in that column by those in column 2a or 2b for those not participating or participating in a prevention program, respectively. Thus, the proportion of all people not participating in a prevention program who will ever try cocaine is calculated by multiplying corresponding quantities in columns 2a and 3 and adding those products (i.e., 0.0168 x 0.5216 + 0.0237 x 0.5171 + ... + 0.4907 x 0.0037 = 0.1774). The proportion of those receiving prevention who try cocaine is analogously estimated by taking this "SUMPRODUCT" of columns 2b and 3, which is 0.1730. Prevention thus reduces cocaine initiation within the cohort receiving the prevention intervention by (0.1774 − 0.1730) / 0.1774, which equals 2.5 percent.

Similarly, the percentage reduction in total cocaine use is calculated by comparing the sum of the products of the elements in columns

2a, 3, and 4 with those in columns 2b, 3, and 4. Most public policy analysis focuses on the present value of streams of future outcomes, not their simple sum. The percentage change in discounted future consumption is calculated in exactly the same way, but substituting the quantities in column 6 for those in column 4.[9] The two values obtained for the discounted totals are 8.31 grams without prevention and 7.99 grams with prevention, yielding a percentage reduction of 3.89 percent. This is the key result emanating from Table 5.1. (For analogous results for other substances and decay and delay assumptions, see Appendix F.) When the percentage reduction is divided by the relevant short-term effectiveness percentage (10.9 percent), the calculation yields a value of 0.357 for Factor 5.[10]

Parallel calculations were conducted for all 12 combinations of substances and initiation scenarios. (As a sensitivity analysis, these calculations were replicated with the alternate decay curves from Appendix E and for the alternate measure of problematic alcohol consumption. Differences were not large and are discussed in Appendix F.)

Results

Values for Factor 5 for all four substances and all three scenarios are reported in Table 5.2. Recall that Factor 5 is the percentage reduction in lifetime consumption per percentage point reduction in end-of-program effectiveness at reducing the predictor variable (typically, initiation). (All results shown are for the primary-model-of-decay assumption. For a graphical presentation of results for alternate decay assumptions, see Appendix F.)

---

[9]Differences between the percentage change in the present value of future consumption and the percentage change in the undiscounted sum of future consumption tend to be very modest.

[10]This is not the same Factor 5 value reported for cocaine in Table 2.2 because that table is based on the conservative initiation delay scenario, whereas Table 5.1 is based on the optimistic scenario. We have used the optimistic scenario here because it is easier to see how the post-prevention drop in initiation is made up later with this scenario than it is with the conservative scenario.

Table 5.2

Values for Factor 5

Substance	Initiation Scenario		
	Conservative	Optimistic	Very Optimistic
Cocaine	27.6%	35.7%	51.2%
Marijuana	16.0%	35.3%	49.0%
Tobacco	14.0%	23.5%	44.2%
Alcohol (Drunkenness)	17.3%	21.2%	31.5%

In reviewing the percentages shown in Table 5.2, several observations emerge:

- First, one should not extrapolate reductions observed at the end of the program to lifetime reductions. With the conservative initiation scenario (our preferred scenario), lifetime reductions are only one-sixth as great as end-of-program initiation reductions for alcohol, tobacco, and marijuana. The corresponding value for cocaine is noticeably larger (a bit above one-quarter), but still much less than one.

- Second, the results are quite sensitive to the initiation delay assumption, but in different ways for different substances. More-optimistic scenarios increase estimated effects on marijuana quite markedly and steadily because people who do not try marijuana until older ages are much less likely to use marijuana heavily than those who start early. For tobacco, the optimistic scenario yields only modestly larger Factor 5 values than does the conservative scenario. However, there is a huge jump when one moves to the very optimistic scenario because under that scenario, many of those whose initiation is deferred through high school never initiate at all. In terms of reducing lifetime cigarette consumption, the key is not delaying initiation but eliminating it altogether because those who start smoking late end up smoking almost as much as those who start early. The trend for cocaine use is similar. Those who initiate marijuana use between ages 19 and 21 historically have used almost as much cocaine as those who initiated marijuana at age 17 or 18, so there is little projected gain in terms of cocaine prevention in moving from the conservative to the optimistic scenario.

- Third, focusing on the conservative initiation scenario (our preferred scenario), one can make a simple but powerful generalization. Roughly speaking, for every 1 percent reduction in use observed at the end of a prevention program, one can anticipate a 0.15 percent reduction in lifetime use of the same substance; or, equivalently, 10 percent reductions at the end of the program suggest 1.5 percent reductions in lifetime use. For cocaine, there is about a 0.25–0.30 percent reduction in lifetime use for every 1 percent observed reduction in marijuana use.

Those with a more optimistic view of initiation delay would bump up these reduction percentages somewhat for tobacco (to about 0.23:1—i.e., 0.23 percent lifetime reduction per 1.0 percent reduction at program completion) and dramatically increase the percentages for marijuana (to 0.35:1), but not increase them as much for cocaine or alcohol (drunkenness). And those who are very optimistic about permanence would use even higher factors (roughly 0.50:1 for cocaine and marijuana, 0.44:1 for tobacco, and 0.32:1 for alcohol [drunkenness]).

Chapter Six

ADJUSTMENTS TO PREVENTION'S EFFECTIVENESS

The result of the calculations described in the three preceding chapters is a set of estimates of average lifetime reduction in drug consumption, one for each substance and for each of three initiation scenarios. The calculation of benefits is completed when such average lifetime use reduction values are multiplied by social cost per unit of substance use. First, though, the use reduction numbers must be adjusted because we have not yet accounted for the following four possibilities:

- That prevention's impact on lifetime use might be less than what is suggested by combining impacts on predictor variables and historical correlations between those predictors and lifetime consumption

- That prevention's effectiveness on predictor variables, as measured to date, will not hold up once the programs are scaled up to serve large numbers of children

- That delaying drug use by some program participants may delay or eliminate drug use by youth who would otherwise have been influenced to initiate drug use by the program participants

- That prevention's shrinking of the market may allow existing enforcement resources to operate more efficiently and, hence, to decrease consumption further.

We account for these four possibilities in this chapter through Factors 6 through 9: the correlation/causation qualifier, the scale-up qualifier, the social multiplier, and the market multiplier, respectively. Because there is little evidence regarding the two qualifiers, our estimates could fairly be described as hypothetical or speculative. However, the values of the qualifiers should not vary with the substance, so our conclusions regarding the distribution of benefits across substances would be unaffected by error in the estimates. Furthermore, just because there is little evidence concerning their magnitude does not mean that the factors are not real, and including them explicitly as factors is an important part of the overall framework for understanding prevention's cost-effectiveness.

Our approach to estimating Factors 6 through 9 generally follows that of Caulkins et al. (1999). For details beyond those provided here, see the appendices to that report.

CAUSATION VERSUS CORRELATION QUALIFIER

The estimate of prevention's effect on lifetime consumption in Factors 4 and 5 is based on its effect on initiation to date (or, for the more optimistic scenarios discussed in Chapter Five, annual prevalence). Initiation is reduced at ages 12 to 14 and is assumed to increase later (if at all). Historically, later initiates have consumed smaller quantities of drugs over the course of their lives. Factors 4 and 5 assume that, by effectively turning early initiates into later initiates, prevention turns people who eventually consume drugs in large quantities into people who consume them in more modest quantities.

Early initiation and eventual consumption *could* be linked in this way. In the extreme, early initiation of marijuana could in itself dispose people toward eventual greater lifetime consumption of marijuana and cocaine. More likely, people may differ in their proclivity toward use of the drug in question (or of drugs in general), so that early initiation of marijuana use and eventual consumption of marijuana and cocaine are both symptoms of that underlying problem. Prevention could work by attenuating the proclivity toward drug use. Delayed initiation of the predictor could be one manifestation of that reduced proclivity; reduced lifetime use could be another.

However, early initiation and eventual consumption need not be so linked. The historical correlation may be only coincidental. It may reflect some demographic or socioeconomic factor rather than an underlying proclivity. To take a hypothetical example, what if male users consumed more marijuana in their lifetime than females did, and boys initiated earlier than girls? It might then be gender that determined lifetime consumption, and the difference in initiation age might be incidental. If so, prevention would still change early initiates into late initiates but it would fail to change heavier lifetime users into more moderate users because it could not change boys into girls.

In reality, neither initiation age, nor gender, nor any other single factor absolutely determines lifetime consumption. The question is, to what extent is a prevention-induced change in initiation translated into a change in lifetime consumption? If the answer is "to the fullest extent," the value of the causation/correlation qualifier, Factor 6, is one. If the answer is "not at all," the value of the qualifier (and of the product of all factors) is zero. We sought to determine where the value most likely falls within that range of zero to one.

To get some sense of the degree to which the connection between initiation age and lifetime consumption might be driven by other variables, Caulkins et al. (1999) broke down the NHSDA sample by variables such as the following: gender, race, neighborhood, ethnicity, initiation age for other substances, census tract income and housing characteristics, and receipt of welfare or food stamps. Caulkins et al. then constructed the correlations between initiation age and lifetime consumption for such subgroups. These analyses suggested qualifier values ranging between 0.89 and 1.00, with one outlier between 0.76 and 0.86. Such estimates are not reassuring, though, if the variable responsible for lifetime consumption were some unmeasured personality characteristic that prevention could not affect. Therefore, in addition to setting our "best guess" Factor 6 value at 0.9, toward the low end of the range of estimates for homogenous subgroups, we adopt for our sensitivity analyses (see Chapter Two) a conservative value of 0.5. For the high end of the range, we take a value of 1.0.

SCALE-UP QUALIFIER

The second qualifier, Factor 7, accounts for possible degradation in effectiveness if the experimental programs upon which we base effectiveness at reducing initiation were scaled up to the state or national level. Such problems with scaling up can occur for a variety of reasons and are not unique to drug prevention. Most significant, experimental demonstrations are usually conducted under the watchful eye of their designers to ensure that the new protocol is being truly and fully implemented. That kind of attention cannot be given once the program is widely adopted.

The ability to design and implement a high-quality intervention does not necessarily imply an ability to disseminate the protocol, and the reasoning behind it, to all adopters. Even if dissemination is flawless, local conditions can influence fidelity to the original design. Implementation can be affected by resource constraints, limitations in teacher quality, and a desire by school administrators or teachers to adapt the curriculum either to local conditions or in response to personal experience and attitudes. Some adaptations may improve effectiveness, but given the relative infrequency with which prevention programs have been shown to work, departures from a model design are more likely to subtract from measured effectiveness rather than add to it.

Despite the potential for degradation of effect on moving from demonstration to widespread adoption, the literature gives almost no guidance as to reasonable numerical estimates. The only source that has even hazarded a guess is Greenwood et al. (1998), the authors of which used a scale-up factor of 0.6 while explicitly admitting the lack of an empirical basis for it. In the absence of any further guesses or any published criticism of the Greenwood et al. study, we adopt the Greenwood value as our "best guess" estimate of Factor 7 and round it down to 0.5 for the lower end of a reasonable range and symmetrically set 0.7 as the upper end.

SOCIAL MULTIPLIER

To the extent that initiation into drug use is a contagious or epidemic phenomenon, preventing one person from initiating may reduce future consumption by a greater amount than that one individual would have consumed. The first person's initiation might, for example, lead through various personal interactions to, ultimately, two other people initiating. Then the expected amount of consumption averted by preventing the first initiation would be about three times the average lifetime consumption of any one individual. We define the total number of initiations prevented per primary initiation to be the "social multiplier," Factor 8. In the example just mentioned, its value would be three.

Caulkins et al. (1999) were solely interested in cocaine, and we reproduce the rationale behind their estimates here. We will then have some words to say about the social multiplier for other substances.

If, as it appears to be the case, most cocaine users are introduced to the drug by a friend or family member, then all other things being equal, the more current users there are, the higher initiation should be. Light users may be the most dynamic proselytizers because, on average, they are relatively recent converts to use themselves and may not yet have experienced many adverse consequences of substance use (Behrens et al., 1999, 2000, 2002).

Over time, drugs create problems for users, and the drugs acquire a reputation for being dangerous. There is no direct measure of either drug reputation or problematic use, but heavy users are more likely to manifest adverse outcomes associated with their use than are light users. This tends to work against recruitment; at the same time, the circle of people who have any interest in drug use and have not already tried the drug is decreasing. Hence, all other things being equal, the greater the "history" of use, and particularly of heavy use, the lower one would expect initiation (overall and per user) to be. The word "history" is used to connote a cumulative process; a reputation is acquired over time. But bad reputations are also not immortal. Musto (1987) hypothesized that upswings of drug use, resulting in a new cycle, arise when current young cohorts, who have not yet experienced or been exposed to the adverse experiences of their older-cohort predecessors, begin using drugs.

The basic outlines of the ways that initiation depends on other variables are clear: Lighter users promote initiation, and more-heavy users or those with a greater accumulated experience with heavy use deter it. What are not clear are the details—how these effects net out, what specific metrics should be used, what mathematical forms the relationships should take, and so on. It is not possible to sort this out experimentally, and relevant historical data are scarce. Hence, the simplified models on which Caulkins et al. (1999) based the social multiplier may well be wrong both in detail (i.e., in their parameter values) and in general (i.e., in their functional form). Nevertheless, they represent the best estimates that can be made at this time; however tenuous, they are probably better than ignoring the social multiplier altogether.

Caulkins et al. found that, across a range of functional forms and parameter values, the social multiplier for cocaine at this stage of the U.S. cocaine epidemic varied between 1.0 and 2.9. We use these two values as the lower and upper ends of a reasonable range, and we take 2.0 as the medium value for calculating a "best-guess" drug prevention benefit.

There has been strikingly little attention paid by researchers to social multiplier effects for other substances. Because any estimates would have to be speculative, we take the conservative approach of assuming no multiplier effect, i.e., that Factor 8 is 1.0 for the other substances. Our comfort level with this value is somewhat enhanced by the tendency of speculation in this regard to suggest a lower multiplier for other substances than for cocaine.

For example, in the case of alcohol and tobacco, use is endemic, not epidemic, so we would not expect to see variations in the social multiplier over time. We might expect that multiplier to be smaller for the licit substances than it is for cocaine, even at the latter's current, late-epidemic level because there are so many nonpeer influences to use licit substances: Their use is seen as "normal"; alcohol, in particular, is widely advertised. And they are so commonly used among youths that the marginal effect of removing some (relatively small) percentage of users through prevention would not seem likely to meaningfully reduce whatever peer pressure exists. It might, however, contribute to active peer pressure against use. Regardless, for substances used by middle-schoolers (alcohol, tobacco, and marijuana, but not cocaine), we might expect a substantial fraction of the peer influences to occur among classmates. These effects should be picked up in the program evaluations, i.e., for classmates there should be no multiplier effect beyond the reductions measured at final follow-up.

While these arguments support a social multiplier less than that for cocaine, they give no clue as to how much less it should be. Thus, for the sake of simplicity and conservatism, we take a multiplier of 1.0.

MARKET MULTIPLIER

As is the case for most goods, the quantity of illicit drugs demanded goes down when the price goes up (Caulkins et al., 1999; Chaloupka and Pacula, 2000). Shrinking the market by removing users (e.g., through prevention) causes the price to go up because it allows the existing enforcement resources to concentrate on a smaller target (Kleiman, 1993). That concentration of resources raises the risks and costs per unit of drug brought to market—risks and costs for which suppliers will want to be compensated monetarily through increased prices (Reuter and Kleiman, 1986). These market effects enhance the impact of any intervention that reduces demand, yielding total soci-etal reductions in use that are a multiple of the reduction in use stemming directly from the intervention. By applying the market multiplier to the estimated effect of a prevention program, we ac-count for the enhanced productivity of a given level of enforcement resources resulting from the interaction between the prevention and enforcement programs. Since the increased enforcement productiv-ity is caused by the prevention program, it is appropriate to consider it a prevention program benefit.

Working from a market model constructed in an earlier study, Caulkins et al. (1999) estimated that the most likely value of the mar-ket multiplier, Factor 9, is 1.38. The interaction with enforcement in-creases prevention's effectiveness by about a third.

The expression of the market multiplier is a function of four parame-ters. Caulkins et al. repeatedly varied each of these four parameters randomly over an assumed distribution (that is, they performed a Monte Carlo simulation) to determine the likelihood that the multi-plier would take different values. The 2.5th and 97.5th percentiles of the resulting distribution of market multiplier values were 1.08 and 2.06, respectively.

These values, however, assume that reduced cocaine demand does not lead to reduced law enforcement effort against the drug. This is probably true for marginal changes in demand over the short run (months), but is false over the long run (years). Redirection of law enforcement effort toward other drugs would reduce or eliminate the market effect (as far as cocaine control is concerned), driving the market multiplier closer to 1. We have no idea how much closer to 1 it is, so we simply round the low, mid-range, and high values for Factor 9 down slightly to 1.0, 1.3, and 2.0. This allows for the possibility that there is no multiplier effect through the market.

For marijuana, a much smaller proportion of the cost structure represents compensation for sanctions, and no comparable story of enforcement concentration can be told for the licit substances. Thus, for the substances other than cocaine, we assume a market multiplier of 1.0, which we do not vary in the sensitivity analyses.

Chapter Seven

SOCIAL COSTS OF DRUG CONSUMPTION

In this chapter, we demonstrate how we estimate the final factor, Factor 10, used in calculating the social benefit from reduction in drug use. Multiplying Factor 4 (see Chapter Four) by Factor 5 (see Chapter Five) yields the percentage reduction in lifetime consumption expected from an average person's participation in prevention. Multiplying that product by Factors 1, 2, and 3 (see Chapter Three) yields the unadjusted present value (e.g., grams) of lifetime consumption by the average program participant that is reduced by prevention. This amount is then adjusted by the application of qualifiers and multipliers (see Chapter Six). The final step in estimating the social cost averted by prevention is to multiply the adjusted reduction in use by the average social cost per unit amount (e.g., a gram) of the substance that is consumed.

We would prefer to calculate the social cost per *marginal* unit of consumption averted, but information about changes in social costs from marginal reductions in use is not available. So, out of necessity, we consider the average, and not the marginal, cost. That is, we implicitly assume that the marginal cost equals the average cost.

Robson and Single (1995) give a useful overview of studies of the social costs of tobacco, alcohol, and illicit drugs. They identified three major methodological approaches: the U.S. Public Health Service's cost-of-illness approach, the external cost approach, and the demographic approach. We focus on the first approach because it is the most widely used and cited, because it is prevalence-based (estimating cost in a given year associated with the substance), and because the results tend to be fairly consistent across studies. An implication of this choice is that some private costs (paid by the user) are included, as well as external costs (paid by others). Specifically, lost life-years are valued based on future earnings. We exclude one private cost (impaired productivity) included in some studies of this type (notably Harwood, Fountain, and Livermore, 1998) because it is not possible to treat it consistently across substances.

Most estimates in the literature and, hence, our figures omit nontangible costs, even those with real economic value. For example, the cost of pain and suffering endured by either the user and/or his or her family is frequently ignored. Similarly, the value of life per se, as distinguished from future expected earnings, is often omitted. Methods are available to evaluate these intangible costs, including estimates of "willingness to pay," but no national estimates have been obtained that could be used to represent these omitted costs for the populations being evaluated.

ESTIMATING THE SOCIAL COST OF ALCOHOL USE

Numerous estimates have been made of the social cost of alcohol abuse (Rice et al., 1990; Harwood et al., 1984; Cruze et al., 1981). The most comprehensive analysis to date is that by Harwood, Fountain, and Livermore (1998), which estimates the annual social cost of alcohol abuse by means of a prevalence-based approach as $148.0 billion in 1992 dollars.[1] We use this study as the basis for our social cost estimates for both alcohol and illicit drugs.

While the Harwood study has been generally praised for its comprehensiveness and methodological improvements over previous studies, criticisms remain regarding the Harwood alcohol cost estimate. For example, a key criticism is the study's reliance on uncertain estimates of the causal link between alcohol use and specific outcomes such as crime (Cohen, 1999). The estimated impact of alcohol use on labor market productivity is also of particular concern (Robson and Single, 1995). Some studies have shown a positive effect on wages (e.g., Cook, 1991; French and Zarkin, 1995) while other studies have shown a negative effect (Mullahy and Sindelar, 1993). Part of this

---

[1]Unless otherwise stated, dollar figures cited in this chapter are annual amounts of consumption or social cost for the United States.

conflict is due to the difficulty in distinguishing moderate alcohol use from heavy use.

We do not count the lost earnings from impaired productivity in our analysis of social cost in part because of these criticisms, but also because there is no defensible way to break down the analogous figure by drug for the illicit drugs. Omitting the lost earnings allows a consistent social cost definition across substances, which is essential when comparing benefits by substance. This omission and the resulting social cost definition is conservative with respect to the conclusion that the social benefits of prevention probably exceed the costs of running the programs. For alcohol $67.7 billion (45.7 percent) of the original estimate was attributable to impaired productivity, so the extent of conservatism may be substantial. Subtracting the impaired productivity costs from Harwood, Fountain, and Livermore's (1998) original figure of $148 billion gives our figure: $80.3 billion in 1992 dollars.

ESTIMATING THE SOCIAL COST OF TOBACCO USE

The cost-of-illness literature on smoking (for example, Chaloupka and Warner, 2000) generally focuses on three main categories of costs:

- The direct medical costs of preventing, diagnosing, and treating smoking-related diseases

- The indirect costs associated with lost earnings because of smoking-related illnesses

- The indirect costs related to the loss of future earnings due to premature smoking-produced deaths.

In contrast with alcohol and illicit drugs, there are not many smoking-related costs from crime, violence, or criminal justice activities. There is no clear consensus estimate of the burden these three listed factors generate, although there is a general consensus that current estimates provided in the literature underestimate the true social cost of smoking for a number of reasons. These reasons include the fact that current studies ignore the following costs:

- Certain categories of smoking-related health care costs, such as treatment of burn victims and/or perinatal care due to low-birth-weight babies

- Costs of treatment of diseases caused by second-hand smoke

- The additional health care costs caused by complications of smoking during the course of various illnesses

- Other nonmedical direct costs, such as time and transportation costs to treatment for smoking-related conditions, damage to buildings due to smoking-produced fires, smoking-related maintenance costs in industrial settings and homes, and the increased frequency of laundering necessitated by smoking.

The largest literature pertains to the medical costs attributable to smoking. In reviewing this literature, Warner et al. (1999) described the consensus figure as 6–8 percent of American personal health expenditures, although they noted that the work of Miller et al. (1999) and Hodgson (1992) suggests that the actual costs may be higher. Nevertheless, to be conservative, we adopt Bartlett et al.'s (1994) figure of $50 billion in 1993 dollars (or 7.1 percent of personal health expenditures).

Productivity losses due to early mortality are significant, but have attracted less attention. Rice et al. (1990), using a methodology consistent with Harwood, Fountain, and Livermore (1998), estimated costs of $53.7 billion in 1980 dollars. Combining the medical and mortality costs yields a total of $177 billion in 2001 dollars.

ESTIMATING THE SOCIAL COST OF COCAINE USE AND USE OF ILLICIT DRUGS IN GENERAL

There are essentially no rigorous and detailed estimates of the social cost of cocaine use or use of any other illicit drug, so we identify proportions of different types of drug-related social costs that might be attributable to cocaine. We then apply those proportions to Harwood, Fountain, and Livermore's (1998) estimates.

We begin with the cost of drug abuse services. The Substance Abuse and Mental Health Services Administration (SAMHSA, 2000c) identified the primary substance of abuse for those entering treatment in

1998. About 30 percent of those seeking treatment and listing a drug other than alcohol cited cocaine as the primary substance of abuse. (Those seeking treatment for alcohol are reflected in the alcohol social cost figure cited earlier.) Not all forms of treatment are equally expensive. After making a rough adjustment for the inequality of treatment cost, the share of all treatment expenses for illicit drugs that are attributable to cocaine may be closer to 37 percent. (See Table 7.1.) Other drug categories are treated in parallel.

The medical consequences of drug use may be apportioned on the basis of data from the Drug Abuse Warning Network, which tracks mentions of substances among emergency room patients and medical examiner cases. Cocaine's share among the major illicit drugs is about 45.3 percent and 41.8 percent, respectively. (See Table 7.2.)

Crime costs may be broken down into lost productivity on the part of perpetrators and victims and social costs, e.g., the costs of the criminal justice system. We apportion some of the productivity losses across drugs on the basis of their contributions to the incarcerated population. Other crime costs (the other productivity losses and social costs) are apportioned on the basis of contributions to the crime rate.

Cocaine and heroin together account for about 36 percent of drug arrests (Office of National Drug Control Policy [ONDCP], 2000), but they account for the majority of expensive incarceration. Exact figures are hard to come by, but Thomas (1998) estimated that marijuana offenders account for only 36,580 (8.7 percent) of the roughly 420,000 people incarcerated for drug offenses (in 1998),[2] and a number of Thomas's approximations would tend to inflate his estimate.[3] Because incarceration costs are much greater than arrest and prose-

---

[2]Maguire and Pastore (2000) reported that there were 55,984 drug offenders in federal prisons. They also reported that 22 percent of jail inmates in 1996 were incarcerated for drug offenses, and 20.7 percent of state prisoners in 1997 were incarcerated for drug offenses. Assuming those fractions can be applied to the 1998 jail and prison populations of 592,462 and 1,129,146, respectively, and adding the federal drug prisoners yields a total of about 420,000 incarcerated for drug offenses.

[3]Thomas's estimates are based on extrapolations from very limited data and rely on a series of assumptions because there are no precise estimates of the number of marijuana offenders in prison or jail or the fraction of those offenders who are truly nonviolent offenders.

Table 7.1

Estimating the Proportion of Treatment Spending, by Type of Illicit Drug

	Heroin or Other Opiates	Cocaine	Marijuana or Hashish	Other Identified Drugs	Total	Cost per Admission (1992 dollars)[a]
Admissions						
Ambulatory	139,320	124,970	167,771	51,419	483,481	$762
Residential or rehabilitation	30,839	68,617	32,970	21,583	154,010	$5,107
Detoxification (24-hour service)	63,348	39,905	7,929	10,221	121,403	$3,400
Total admissions	233,507	233,493	208,671	83,224	758,895	—
Proportion of admissions	30.8%	30.8%	27.5%	11.0%	100.0%	—
Weighted cost (millions of 1992 dollars)	$479	$581	$323	$184	$1,568	—
Proportion of costs	30.6%	37.1%	20.6%	11.7%	100.0%	—

NOTE: Slight discrepancies between the individual entries and their sums are due to rounding.

[a] Ambulatory and residential/rehabilitation-treatment costs are from Rydell and Everingham (1994). Current costs for detoxification are on the order of $4,000 (Kott and Nottingham, 1999), which is approximately $3,400 per admission in 1992 dollars.

cution costs, this analysis suggests that the vast majority of criminal justice costs are associated with cocaine and heroin. The exact division between cocaine and heroin is hard to know, in part because of how some criminal justice data are tabulated, but the ONDCP (2000, p. 116) estimated that three-quarters of those who were "hard core" users of either cocaine or heroin were hard core cocaine users.

Recognizing that some people are incarcerated for use and distribution of drugs other than cocaine and heroin, one might infer that roughly two-thirds of drug-related incarceration in the United States pertains to cocaine. We apply the same proportion to determine cocaine's proportion of earnings lost by those in residential treatment or forcibly confined to a behavioral-health facility.

Most drug-related crime is driven by drug expenditures, either because the crime is committed to finance a user's drug purchase or a crime is committed during a conflict over the revenues or profits of the drug sales. The ONDCP (2000) estimated that in 1998 cocaine accounted for just under 60 percent of total expenditures for illicit drugs. Cocaine's share of drug-related crime is probably higher than 60 percent, though, because marijuana's share of drug-related crime

Table 7.2

Estimating Cocaine's Share of Morbidity- and Mortality-Related Costs

Substance	Number of Emergency Department Mentions (1999)[a]	Proportion of Mentions	Number of Mentions by Medical Examiners (1999)[b]	Proportion of Mentions
Cocaine	168,764	45.3%	4,864	41.8%
Heroin	84,408	22.6%	4,820	41.4%
Marijuana	87,150	23.4%	670	5.8%
Methamphetamine	10,447	2.8%	690	5.9%
Amphetamine	11,954	3.2%	452	3.9%
PCP	4,969	1.3%	98	0.8%
LSD	5,126	1.4%	—	—
Fentanyl	—	—	53	0.5%
Total	372,818	100%	11,647	100%

[a]Source: SAMHSA (2000d), p. 99.
[b]Source: SAMHSA (2000a), p. 39.

is almost certainly smaller than its one-sixth share of drug-related spending. As Boyum and Kleiman (2001) noted, "Of the three major illicit drugs of abuse (marijuana, cocaine, and heroin), one would expect marijuana to be the least implicated in crime." Indeed, in Tonry and Wilson's (1990) venerable volume on *Drugs and Crime*, marijuana does not even appear in the index. Even if we generously assume that marijuana generates one-third as much crime per dollar as do cocaine, heroin, and the other illicit drugs, marijuana's share of crime-related costs would be only 6 percent, and therefore cocaine's share may be more like 67 percent. (See Table 7.3.) This percentage is applied to earnings lost by both criminals on the street and victims and to crime's social costs.

In Table 7.4, we show the results of applying these various proportions to the broad categories of economic costs of drug abuse listed by Harwood, Fountain, and Livermore (1998) to estimate that cocaine's share of these social costs was 59 percent or about $49 billion. Parallel calculations show that marijuana's share was something less than 9 percent ($7 billion), and heroin/opiates' share was 25 percent ($21 billion). All other drugs combined account for the remaining 7 percent ($6 billion). This is an exceedingly rough calculation, made palatable only by the recognition that social cost estimates are in-

Table 7.3

Estimating Cocaine's Share of Drug-Related Crime

Substance	Spending ($billions)[a]	Proportion of Spending	Crime Multiplier[b]	Crime-Driving Force[c]	Estimated Proportion of Crime[d]
Cocaine	39.0	59.3%	1	39.0	66.5%
Heroin	11.6	17.6%	1	11.6	19.8%
Methamphetamine	2.2	3.3%	1	2.2	3.8%
Marijuana	10.7	16.3%	1/3	3.57	6.1%
Other	2.3	3.5%	1	2.3	3.9%
Total	65.8	100.0%	—	58.7	100.0%

[a]Source: ONDCP (2000).
[b]Crimes per dollar spent on a drug, as a fraction of crimes per dollar spent on cocaine.
[c]Spending times crime multiplier.
[d]Crime-driving force as a percentage of total crime-driving force (58.7).

Table 7.4

Apportioning Harwood, Fountain, and Livermore's Social Costs of Drug Use by Drug

	Cost for All Drugs ($billions)	Cocaine	Marijuana or Hashish	Heroin or Other Opiates	All Other Drugs (Residual)	Justification or Nature of Cost
Health Care Expenditures						
Alcohol and drug abuse services	$4.40	37.1%	20.6%	30.6%	11.7%	Pertains primarily to treatment
Medical consequences	$5.53	45.3%	23.4%	22.6%	8.7%	Reflects morbidity
Productivity Impacts (Lost Earnings)						
Premature death	$14.58	41.8%	5.8%	41.4%	11.1%	Based on medical examiner data
Impaired productivity						Excluded
Institutionalized populations[a]	$1.48	66.7%	8.7%	22.2%	2.4%	Share of incarceration
Incarceration	$17.91	66.7%	8.7%	22.2%	2.4%	Share of incarceration
Crime careers[b]	$19.20	66.5%	6.1%	19.8%	7.7%	Modified share of drug expenditures
Victims of crime	$2.06	66.5%	6.1%	19.8%	7.7%	Modified share of drug expenditures

Table 7.4—Continued

	Cost for All Drugs ($billions)	Cocaine	Marijuana or Hashish	Heroin or Other Opiates	All Other Drugs (Residual)	Justification or Nature of Cost
			Other Impacts on Society			
Crime[c]	$17.97	66.5%	6.1%	19.8%	7.7%	Modified share of drug expenditures
Social welfare administration	$0.34	57.1%	20.6%	30.6%	11.7%	Pertains primarily to treatment
Total ($billions in 1992)	$83.5	$49.3	$7.2	$20.8	$6.1	—
Share	—	59.1%	8.6%	24.9%	7.3%	—

[a]Earnings lost by those in residential treatment or forcibly confined to behavioral-health facilities.

[b]Earnings lost by criminals on the street (net of earnings from crime).

[c]Costs of the criminal justice system, of private security systems, of property lost to theft, and of medical treatment of victims.

evitably rough, the number of significant digits to which they are reported notwithstanding.

ESTIMATING THE SOCIAL COST OF MARIJUANA USE

The apportionment exercise conducted in the previous section is more tenuous for marijuana than it is for the other drugs, in part because marijuana less frequently is the sole or even principal cause of very specific harms (e.g., overdose deaths). The scientific literature has demonstrated virtually no interest in developing an estimate of the overall social cost of marijuana use, and very limited research exists on which we could even try to develop such an estimate directly. Hence, we use the figure shown in Table 7.4 ($7.2 billion in 1992, or 8.6 percent of drug-related social costs). However, this estimate should be understood to be even less precise than are the corresponding estimates for the other substances. That is not a problem for this report, in which the main finding concerning marijuana's social costs is that they represent a very modest fraction of prevention's drug-related benefits. Even if marijuana's social costs were double the figure used here, that conclusion would not be threatened. However, it would be inappropriate to use this estimate for many other purposes, as a brief discussion of its limitations will make clear.

In a recent editorial in *Addiction*, Wayne Hall and Thomas Babor (2000) suggested that two factors contribute to the general lack of scientific information on which to base an estimate of marijuana's social costs:

- Marijuana use, although rising in frequency and duration among youth cohorts, is currently only used intermittently and for short time periods during the life course.

- There are insufficient studies to generate a scientific consensus on the toxicity and harmful effects of chronic and/or heavy episodic use of marijuana.

These two factors make examination of marijuana use and abuse less compelling than other legal and illicit substances for which there are more obvious and known public health effects. Nonetheless, Hall and Babor (2000) argued that the case can be made for researchers to take the public health costs of marijuana use seriously. First, they argued that even though only a small proportion of marijuana users adopt patterns of use that pose health risks (one in ten according to Hall, Johnston, and Donnelly, 1999), the growing prevalence of regular marijuana users suggests that the actual number of problem users is on the rise. Second, they believed that there is sufficient scientific evidence to suggest probable adverse health consequences related to both acute intoxication and chronic use of marijuana, including motor vehicle accidents, dependence, respiratory diseases, schizophrenia, and cognitive impairment. As the number of problem users rises, we should expect to see an increase in these negative health outcomes as well.

Methodologically, the biggest difficulty in linking marijuana use to particular health conditions or other societal outcomes is the fact that a large fraction of marijuana users also use other substances (tobacco, alcohol, or other illicit drugs), making the effect that can be attributable to marijuana itself difficult to identify. Scientific data linking marijuana use to specific acute and chronic health conditions are relatively weak. One unusual exception is a study by Polen et al. (1993) that identified 452 daily marijuana smokers who never smoked tobacco. The health service utilization for these daily marijuana smokers was compared with the utilization of nonsmokers in the same health maintenance organization. Even after adjusting for sex, age, race, education, marital status, and alcohol consumption, the marijuana smokers had a 19 percent increased risk of outpatient visits for respiratory illnesses, a 32 percent increased risk of injury, and a 9 percent increased risk of other illnesses as compared with nonsmokers. The daily marijuana users were also 50 percent more likely to be admitted to the hospital.

This study provides perhaps the strongest evidence that marijuana use by itself, independent of tobacco use, may be associated with poor health outcomes and greater health care utilization. Nonetheless, this does not establish causation attributable to marijuana use, and it would be a great leap to assume that marijuana's share of overall morbidity costs could be approximated by its share of emergency department mentions. The vast majority of marijuana-related emergency department episodes also involve other substances (even more so than for other drugs). There is evidence to suggest that marijuana use brings negative health consequences that can require use of expensive health services, but the estimate in Table 7.4 is exceptionally rough.

There is similar confusion concerning mental health care costs associated with marijuana treatment. It is clear from the Treatment Episodes Data Set (TEDS) that treatment admissions with marijuana as the primary substance of abuse have grown rapidly, nearly doubling from 111,265 admissions in 1993 to 208,671 admissions in 1998 (SAMHSA, 2000c). Whether these new admissions are due to a true increase in the number of dependent users has yet to be determined, but such a notion is highly suspect in light of the fact that over half of all marijuana admissions in 1998 were referred from the criminal justice system. These treatment admissions may represent diversion of marijuana offenders from other criminal sanctions, a possibility that creates incentives for dependence to be diagnosed even where it is absent. Nonetheless, there are real economic costs associated with processing and treating this higher caseload. These costs, however, are likely to be significantly less than those for treating cocaine or alcohol dependence because the nature of marijuana dependency is inherently different. Table 7.1 above assumed that treatment costs are the same per admission within a broad modality regardless of the primary substance of abuse, and that is unlikely to be the case.

Perhaps the marijuana cost category studied most extensively is the one excluded in this study, namely productivity impacts. A quick review of the literature shows how little consensus there is concerning these estimates and, hence, why they are excluded here.

There is some evidence that marijuana use itself imposes a cost. Using the 1984 and 1985 waves of the National Longitudinal Survey of Youth (NLSY), Kandel and Davies (1990) found that past-year marijuana use is positively associated with the total number of weeks a user is unemployed even after controlling for cocaine use. Register and Williams (1992) found what would appear to be a conflicting result using data from the 1984 NLSY: Use of marijuana on the job in the past year and long-term use of marijuana are found to have a *positive* impact on the probability of being employed. However, there are plausible explanations for these mixed findings including differences in the set of controls included in the models. Further, both studies treat educational attainment and occupational choice as independent variables unaffected by marijuana use.

Research shows that there is a significant correlation between marijuana use and poor grades (Bachman, Johnston, and O'Malley, 1998; Marston et al., 1998; Dozier and Barnes, 1997), failed classes, suspensions and expulsions from school (Shannon et al., 1993), and dropping out of school (Mensch and Kandel, 1988; Ellickson et al., 1998; Yamada, Kendix, and Yamada, 1996). Other research shows a strong correlation between occupational choice and substance use behavior in general (Kenkel and Wang, 1998). Given that educational attainment and occupational choice have been established as important determinants of wages and other labor market outcomes (Becker, 1964; Mincer, 1970), it is important to consider the indirect effect marijuana use might have on labor market outcomes through these intermediate variables. These types of analyses have yet to be conducted, however.

All of the above suggests that there are real economic costs associated with marijuana use, but it also points out the difficulties in trying to estimate what those costs are.

SUMMARY

Table 7.5 summarizes our assumptions about the social costs per year, by substance. To generate Factor 10, we convert these estimates into the average estimated social cost per unit of use, where use is measured in the units with which we estimate lifetime consumption. To make the conversion, we divide the annual social cost by an estimate of the annual use across the United States. For tobacco, we use data from the Centers for Disease Control (2000) on cigarette consumption in 1999. For marijuana, the ONDCP (2000) provides estimates of consumption in 1992. For cocaine, we use Everingham and Rydell's (1994) estimate of 291 metric tons of consumption in 1992 because our estimate of lifetime cocaine consumption per user is ultimately calibrated to that level of use. For alcohol, we assume that the social costs estimated earlier in this chapter are associated with heavy or problematic use. There are no good data on the number of actual instances of heavy drinking, so we denominate cost per in-

Table 7.5

Summary of Assumed Social Costs per Year by Substance

Substance	Social Cost Estimate	Cost in 2001 ($billions)	Amount of Use in Base Year (1992)	Cost per Unit of Use in 2001 Dollars
Tobacco	$53.7 billion in 1980; $50 billion in 1993	177.2	21.75 billion packs of cigarettes	$8.15 per pack of cigarettes
Alcohol	$148.0 billion – $67.7 billion = $80.4 billion in 1992	101.9	1.834 billion self-reported instances of consuming five or more drinks	$55.60 per self-reported instance of consuming five or more drinks in one sitting
			1.039 billion self-reported instances of drunkenness	$98.10 per self-reported instance of getting drunk
Cocaine	$49.3 billion in 1992	62.6	291 metric tons	$215.20 per gram
Marijuana	$7.2 billion in 1992	9.1	761 metric tons	$12.00 per gram
Heroin	$20.8 billion in 1992	26.4	11.7 metric tons	$2,255 per gram
Other illicit drugs	$6.1 billion in 1992	7.8	—	—

stance of heavy drinking self-reported in the National Household Survey on Drug Abuse (NHSDA).[4]

It is also of interest to note how the dominant components of these social cost estimates vary by substance. As Table 7.6 shows, two-thirds of the social costs of tobacco use (that are accounted for here) stem from lost productivity of smokers who die prematurely. Productivity losses from premature death likewise account for almost 40 percent of the measured social costs of alcohol use, but only 12 percent of the measured social costs of cocaine or marijuana use. In contrast, crime accounts in one way or another for 80 percent of the social costs associated with cocaine, perhaps one-sixth of alcohol-related social costs, and essentially none of the tobacco-related costs. Some people might take the position that crime-related costs are "real" social costs, whereas lost productivity from premature death is a private cost that should not be counted.[5] If so, they would discount most of prevention's smoking-related benefits, but little of its cocaine-related benefits, substantially affecting their conclusions about the proportion of prevention benefits that are attributable to the various substances.

The ten factors described in this chapter and in Chapters Three through Six were combined as explained in Chapter Two to produce our overall results and conclusions, which are presented in Chapter Two (and detailed in brief in the Summary). Further details concerning some of the factors are in the appendices.

---

[4]These alcohol estimates should thus not be construed as accurate estimates of the social cost per instance of heavy drinking. Presumably, such episodes are under-represented to some unknown degree in the NHSDA, which would inflate the apparent estimated cost per episode. But in our social benefit estimate, we multiply that number by the reduction in self-reported instances of heavy drinking, which would be understated proportionally. Any underreporting thus states the estimate in two ways that cancel each other.

[5]The strict version of this position is not sustainable. Lost productivity means lost tax revenues to the government, which is a social cost. Persons who die early also rob society of whatever socially productive value their leisure time may have been worth, e.g., through their volunteer work.

Table 7.6

Dominant Types of Social Costs by Substance

	Tobacco	Alcohol	Cocaine	Marijuana or Hashish	Heroin or Other Opiates	All Other Illicit Drugs
Health care expenditures[a]	35%					
Alcohol and drug abuse services	—	7%	3%	13%	6%	8%
Medical consequences	—	16%	5%	18%	6%	8%
Productivity impacts (lost earnings)	—	—	—	—	—	—
Premature death	65%	39%	12%	12%	29%	26%
Impaired productivity[b]	—	—	—	—	—	—
Institutionalized populations	—	2%	2%	2%	2%	1%
Incarceration	—	7%	24%	22%	19%	7%
Crime careers	—	—	26%	16%	18%	24%
Victims of crime	—	1%	3%	2%	2%	3%
Other impacts on society						
Crime	—	8%	24%	15%	17%	22%
Social welfare administration	—	1%	0%	1%	0%	1%
Motor vehicle crashes	—	17%	N/A	N/A	N/A	N/A
Fire destruction	N/A	2%	N/A	N/A	N/A	N/A

NOTE: N/A = not available.

[a] Health care expenditures for tobacco are not broken down by subcategory in the original source materials.

[b] As noted earlier, we exclude impaired productivity, which is included in some studies of this type, because it is not possible to treat it consistently across substances.

LOW, MEDIUM, AND HIGH ESTIMATES FOR THE TEN FACTORS IN THE PREVENTION MODEL

For purposes of the Monte Carlo simulations presented in Chapter Two, Table A.1 on the next two pages lists the range of values for all ten factors used in calculating prevention's social benefits for each of the five lifetime consumption measures. For Factor 5, percentage reduction in lifetime use per unit of short-term effectiveness, values are given for the conservative, more optimistic, and very optimistic initiation scenarios.

Note: In the cross-substance sensitivity simulation in Chapter Two, only medium values were used for the parameters whose values are identical across substances. If the values of any of those parameters are varied by the same amount and in the same direction across substances, there is no effect on the *relative* contributions to social cost savings by substance. While our medium estimates may be too low or too high, it is likely that, if we are off on one parameter value for one substance, we are off by a similar amount and in the same direction for other substances. The parameters with identical values for the purpose of the simulation are the correlation-causation qualifier, scale-up qualifier, social multiplier, and discount factor. We also use only the medium values for the market multiplier, for which only one substance varies from all the others.

Table A.1

Ranges of Factor Values Used for Calculating Social Value of Prevention for All Five Lifetime Measures

	Cocaine	Marijuana	Tobacco	Alcohol: Self-Reports of Drunkenness	Alcohol: Five or More Drinks at One Sitting
Lifetime Use per Initiate Without Prevention					
Low	225 grams	379 grams	7,826 packs of cigarettes	444 times	775 times
Medium	350 grams	559 grams	8,873 packs of cigarettes	639 times	1,189 times
High	475 grams	876 grams	9,667 packs of cigarettes	894 times	1,606 times
Proportion of Cohort Initiating Without Prevention					
Low	12%	53%	70%	47%	47%
Medium	18%	61.5%	77.5%	58%	58%
High	24%	70%	85%	69%	69%
Discount factor	0.532	0.580	0.419	0.489	0.468
Prevention's End-of-Program Effectiveness on Predictor					
Low	4.9%	4.9%	4.3%	1.7%	1.7%
Medium	10.9%	10.9%	16.8%	12.8%	12.8%
High	14.0%	14.0%	21.5%	30.8%	30.8%
Reduction in Lifetime Use per Unit of Reduction in Predictor Measure					
Conservative scenario					
Low	26.2%	15.7%	12.4%	13.2%	10.4%
Medium	27.6%	16.0%	14.0%	17.3%	14.2%
High	31.6%	18.7%	14.5%	21.8%	19.1%
Optimistic scenario					
Low	35.0%	33.8%	22.4%	17.4%	18.8%
Medium	35.7%	35.3%	23.5%	21.2%	23.5%
High	38.4%	39.9%	23.9%	23.9%	27.7%
Very optimistic scenario					
Low	49.2%	46.5%	42.0%	25.7%	28.1%
Medium	51.2%	49.0%	44.2%	31.5%	35.3%
High	57.2%	56.5%	45.5%	36.7%	42.3%

Table A.1—Continued

	Cocaine	Marijuana	Tobacco	Alcohol: Self-Reports of Drunkenness	Alcohol: Five or More Drinks at One Sitting
Correlation/Causation Ratio					
Low	0.5	0.5	0.5	0.5	0.5
Medium	0.9	0.9	0.9	0.9	0.9
High	1.0	1.0	1.0	1.0	1.0
Scale-Up Factor					
Low	0.5	0.5	0.5	0.5	0.5
Medium	0.6	0.6	0.6	0.6	0.6
High	0.7	0.7	0.7	0.7	0.7
Social Multiplier					
Low	1.0[a]	1.0	1.0	1.0	1.0
Medium	2.0[a]	1.0	1.0	1.0	1.0
High	2.9[a]	1.0	1.0	1.0	1.0
Market Multiplier					
Low	1.0	1.0	1.0	1.0	1.0
Medium	1.3	1.0	1.0	1.0	1.0
High	2.0	1.0	1.0	1.0	1.0
Social cost per unit of use	$215.18	$11.97	$8.15	$98.14	$55.59

[a]This low value for cocaine is used in the worst-case analysis and all three values are used in the analysis of the sensitivity of total prevention benefits. For the analysis of the sensitivity of the allocation of benefits across substances, cocaine's social multiplier is assumed to be an invariant 1.0.

Appendix B
RECODING CONSUMPTION VALUES FROM THE
NATIONAL HOUSEHOLD SURVEY ON DRUG ABUSE

As explained in Chapter Three, the National Household Survey on Drug Abuse (NHSDA) provides data for two of the three estimates of lifetime marijuana use, tobacco use, and heavy alcohol consumption. We aggregate these numbers across users and report consumption as a continuous variable—grams of marijuana, number of packs of cigarettes smoked, self-reported instances of drunkenness. The NHSDA variables are days of marijuana use, number of cigarettes smoked, and number of days on which the respondent reported getting drunk. We assume the last of these is equivalent to instances of drunkenness, and we convert the other two to our preferred usage units, as indicated in Chapter Three.

In all but one case, however, the NHSDA variable is categorical, not continuous. That is, the survey asks about use in sets of consecutive ranges (see the "Meaning" column in Table B.1). Therefore, before we attempt any aggregation or conversion, we need to recode the NHSDA variable from ranges to point estimates. To do this, we take the midpoint of the ranges. Recodings are presented in Tables B.1, B.2, and B.3 for the NHSDA variables *MJYRFREQ* (frequency of marijuana use in the past year), *AVCIG* (number of cigarettes smoked per day), and *DRUNKYR* (number of days of being drunk in the past year).

An alternate measure of problem alcohol consumption—the number of times a respondent reports having had at least five drinks on one occasion—was treated slightly differently. Respondents were asked to report this measure with reference to the past month, and the number of times was recorded as a continuous integer variable. Hence, we simply multiplied that number by 12 to obtain an estimate of the number of times five or more drinks were consumed at one sitting in the past year.

Table B.1

Recoding of NHSDA MJYRFREQ Variable

MJYRFREQ Value	Meaning	Coded as This Number of Days
1	More than 300 days (every day or almost every day)	333
2	201 to 300 days (5 to 6 days a week)	250
3	101 to 200 days (3 to 4 days a week)	150
4	51 to 100 days (1 to 2 days a week)	75
5	25 to 50 days (3 to 4 days a month)	38
6	12 to 24 days (1 to 2 days a month)	18
7	6 to 11 days (less than one day a month)	9
8	3 to 5 days in the past 12 months	4
9	1 to 2 days in the past 12 months	1.5
Other valid values	0 days in the past 12 months	0

Table B.2

Recoding of NHSDA AVCIG Variable

AVCIG Value	Meaning	Coded as This Number of Cigarettes
1	At least one puff but less than one cigarette each day	0.5
2	1 to 5 cigarettes each day	3
3	6 to 15 cigarettes (about 1/2 pack) each day	10
4	16 to 25 cigarettes (about 1 pack) each day	20
5	26 to 35 cigarettes (about 1-1/2 packs) each day	30
6	35 or more cigarettes (about 2 packs) each day	40
Other valid values	None	0

Table B.3

Recoding of NHSDA DRUNKYR Variable

DRUNKYR Value	Meaning	Coded as This Number of Days
1	More than 300 days (every day or almost every day)	333
2	201 to 300 days (5 to 6 days a week)	250
3	101 to 200 days (3 to 4 days a week)	150
4	51 to 100 days (1 to 2 days a week)	75
5	25 to 50 days (3 to 4 days a month)	38
6	12 to 24 days (1 to 2 days a month)	18
7	6 to 11 days (less than one day a month)	9
8	3 to 5 days in the past 12 months	4
9	1 to 2 days in the past 12 months	1.5
Other valid values	0 days in the past 12 months	0

PROGRAM DESCRIPTIONS

This appendix presents background information on the various pre-vention programs examined for this study—the Lifeskills program, Midwest Prevention Project, Project Northland, Iowa Strengthening Families Program, Project ALERT, the enhanced Alcohol Misuse Prevention Study, and Project TNT (Toward No Tobacco Use).

LIFESKILLS

Lifeskills (Botvin et al., 1995) was evaluated in a longitudinal, ran-domized trial of 56 public schools, each of which received one of the following: a comprehensive school-based prevention program with provider training workshops and ongoing consultation, the preven-tion program with videotaped training and no consultation, or nothing (the control group). The target group was seventh- to twelfth-graders; seventh-graders were enrolled, and they followed through with the program through the twelfth grade. The retention rate was 60 percent, for a final sample size of 3,597. Target race/ ethnicity was mixed, but the actual sample predominantly was white.

The key prevention strategy was prevention education with training in resistance skills and in generic personal and social skills. The ob-jective was to reduce substance use in terms of current use (past week and past 30 days) of alcohol, tobacco, marijuana, and multiple drugs; frequency of pack-per-day cigarette smoking and heavy drinking (three-plus drinks at a time); and prevalence of monthly drunkenness. The program was implemented by regular classroom teachers. It consisted of 15 sessions conducted over one year, with ten booster sessions in the eighth grade and five booster sessions in the ninth grade. The evaluation used a pre-post design with a comparison group, measured in twelfth grade, six years after the start of the program start. Results for the two experimental groups are combined. We did not treat the program's "high-fidelity" sample separately in our analysis.

MIDWEST PREVENTION PROJECT (MPP)

MPP was a six-year community-based intervention that included mass-media, school-based (Project STAR), parent-education, and community components. It was implemented in 42 schools in 15 communities within the Kansas City metropolitan area beginning in 1984. The target group consisted of youths in the sixth and seventh grades of mixed race/ethnicity; 79 percent of the final sample was white, 17 percent was African-American, 2 percent was Hispanic, and 3 percent was of another race/ethnicity.

Key prevention strategies were information dissemination and prevention education with resistance-skills training. The objectives of the program included delaying onset of use and reducing and preventing past-week and 30-day use of alcohol, tobacco, and marijuana. The school-based portion of the program was implemented by regular classroom teachers. There were ten youth-education sessions plus ten homework assignments conducted over 1.5 years. The study design was quasi-experimental; schools were assigned to a treatment or control group based on scheduling flexibility. The evaluation was a pre-post design.

PROJECT NORTHLAND

Project Northland was aimed principally at reducing alcohol use among youths in the sixth through eighth grades. The program was implemented in rural northern Minnesota, with a predominantly (95 percent) white sample. The program was multifaceted, with the key prevention strategies being information dissemination to parents of sixth-graders, prevention education with resistance-skills training, alternative drug-free activities, and community-based intervention (including passage of local ordinances to make it difficult for youths to obtain alcohol).

School was the primary setting for the program, although parents were involved through homework assignments. Indicators included any use (tobacco), annual use (marijuana and multiple drugs), and past-week and 30-day use (alcohol). The program was implemented by research staff, regular classroom teachers, and peer leaders. Components included a comprehensive school-based program, a parent program, and involvement by community organizations and churches. Twenty sessions were conducted over three years, with four sessions in the sixth grade, eight sessions in the seventh grade, and eight sessions in the eighth grade. The design was pre-post with a comparison group, with follow-ups at the end of sixth, seventh, and eighth grades. A twelfth-grade follow-up was also planned, but data on that follow-up are not yet available as of this writing.

IOWA STRENGTHENING FAMILIES

The target group in the Iowa Strengthening Families program consisted of youths in the sixth grade. Schools were randomized, although the intervention occurred within the family. Families of all sixth-graders enrolled at 22 rural schools were recruited for participation in either an experimental group that included a seven-session program or a control group; 238 families were in the program, and 238 were in the control group.

The key prevention strategy was prevention education along with resistance-skills training. The objective of the program was delaying the onset of alcohol use. The measure used in the evaluation was someone ever having used alcohol. The program also had a parent component, which included the skills-training sessions and ten homework assignments over 1-1/3 years. For the children, there were seven sessions over a seven-week period. Follow-ups occurred at the end of years 1 and 2 following the program.

PROJECT ALERT

The Project ALERT curriculum is based on the social-influence model. It helps students to develop reasons not to use drugs, to identify and counter pressures to use drugs, to understand that most people do not use drugs, and to recognize the benefits of resistance. The evaluated trial was conducted from 1983 to 1986. Thirty schools in California and Oregon participated, representing urban, suburban, and rural settings. Nine schools had a "minority" population of 50 percent or more of the student body, and 18 were in neighborhoods with family incomes below the state median. Ten schools were monitored as controls.

In the 20 treatment schools, an eight-session curriculum was given to seventh-graders. The following year, three booster sessions were given. Multiple measures (daily, weekly, monthly, past-month, and past-year use and lifetime prevalence) were made of marijuana, alcohol, and tobacco use, along with heavy-use measures of the two licit substances. These measurements were taken in the eighth, ninth, and twelfth grades.

ENHANCED ALCOHOL MISUSE PREVENTION STUDY

The Alcohol Misuse Prevention Study (AMPS) consisted of four sessions training fifth- and sixth-grade students to resist social pressures to use alcohol. A subsequent enhanced version of the AMPS curriculum began in the sixth grade but doubled the number of sessions to eight; it included five additional sessions in the seventh grade and four in the eighth grade and allowed for more active student participation. The enhanced AMPS was carried out in seven southeastern Michigan school districts. School buildings were matched by test scores and ethnicity and then randomly assigned to treatment or control conditions. The curriculum was administered in the winter of 1990. Students had been pretested in the fall and were posttested in the spring and again in the spring of seventh and eighth grades. Testing included questions about frequency and quantity of alcohol use, as well as "misuse," as measured by drunkenness, sickness, or trouble with peers and adults related to alcohol (Shope et al., 1994).

PROJECT TNT

Project TNT (Toward No Tobacco Use) was a ten-day social influence plus physical consequences curriculum delivered to seventh-graders in a controlled trial involving 6,716 students from 48 junior high schools, 60 percent of whom were non-Hispanic white, 27 percent were Latino, 7 percent were African-American, and 6 percent were Asian-American. Information was available from one- and two-year follow-ups that monitored lifetime prevalence and weekly use. Project TNT is premised on the theory that youths will be able to resist tobacco products if they (1) are aware of misleading social information that facilitates tobacco use, (2) have skills to counteract social pressures, and (3) appreciate the physical consequences tobacco use can have.

AGGREGATING PROGRAM EFFECTIVENESS DATA

In this appendix, we demonstrate how we aggregated the program effectiveness data reported by the evaluations of various prevention programs into the numbers given in Table 4.5. First, we use Project ALERT as an example to demonstrate our approach to aggregating program data across various user types and treatment groups into a single number for each effectiveness measure, as reported in Tables 4.2, 4.3, and 4.4. Then, we detail our methods for aggregating the numbers in those tables across programs.

INDIVIDUAL PROGRAM EFFECTIVENESS

Project ALERT's evaluation design consists of youths from three different risk groups being allocated to one of two different treatment groups (teen leader versus health educator leader) or one control group in the beginning of the study.[1] The three risk groups in the case of marijuana are as follows: (1) youth who are nonusers of tobacco and marijuana at baseline, (2) youth who are nonusers of marijuana but users of tobacco at baseline, and (3) youth who are marijuana users at baseline. Program effects and measures of use are

---

[1]Lifeskills similarly had two different treatment groups that had to be aggregated. We followed a similar procedure for aggregating across the two different treatment groups. Lifeskills did not separately identify baseline users, however, so the aggregation process was considerably simpler. We also followed the ALERT procedure as it was pertinent to the Enhanced AMPS program, which did not have different treatment groups but identified three different baseline types of drinkers in its treatment and control groups: those who have always abstained from drinking alcohol, those who have drunk alcohol but only in the presence of an adult, and those who have drunk alcohol in an unsupervised setting.

presented for each of these risk groups and treatment/control groups separately. Given that two different treatment groups are evaluated in Project ALERT with three different baseline risk categories of users, it is useful to discuss how this and the other composite indicators from Project ALERT were calculated.

As Table D.1 illustrates, for any given follow-up measure (we use lifetime prevalence as an example), we used the following steps:

1. We began by taking the simple unweighted average of the follow-up measure across the two treatment groups ([teen leader measure + adult leader measure]/2).

   It was necessary to use the unweighted average because we did not actually know the number of youths in each baseline category who were allocated among the two treatment groups and the control group. We did not feel that this was a problem in light of

Table D.1

Estimation of Project ALERT Composite Program Effect on Marijuana Initiation

	Baseline Nonusers	Baseline Tobacco Users	Total
Size of Group	1,976	1,344	—
Step 1: Calculate average follow-up measure			
Treatment Group 1 (Teen Leader): Lifetime prevalence	8.3%	31.9%	—
Treatment Group 2 (Health Educator): Lifetime prevalence	8.3%	31.0%	—
Average of treatment group	8.3%	31.45%	—
Step 2: Calculate weighted average for treatment and control groups			
Control group: Lifetime prevalence	12.1%	28.1%	—
Number initiating under treatment condition (T)	164	423	587
Number initiating under control condition (C)	239	378	617
Step 3: Calculate weighted average difference across baseline user groups [(C–T)/C]	31.4%	–11.9%	4.9%

NOTE: The study also included baseline marijuana users, whose initiation rates were by definition 100 percent in both treatment and control groups and who were thus omitted from this analysis.

the fact that there were only small differences in reported use rates across the two types of treatment groups.

2. Next, we multiplied this average and the corresponding percentage for the control group by the group size to obtain the number of youths who would initiate with and without prevention in each group; we then summed across groups.

3. We then calculated the percentage difference in the total number of youths initiating marijuana use between control and treatment conditions. The percentage change in the total number of initiators is the estimate of the short-term program effectiveness.

AGGREGATE PROGRAM EFFECTIVENESS

Before proceeding to construct our composite program effectiveness parameters, we flag three issues related to developing aggregate performance measures:

1. Many of the measures presented in Tables 4.2 through 4.4 (reproduced here as Tables D.2, D.3, and D.4) can be shown to be risk factors for subsequent alcohol, tobacco, marijuana, and cocaine use. However, we need measures corresponding to those in the National Household Survey on Drug Abuse (NHSDA) for all the measures in Tables D.2, D.3, and D.4; the only measures that correspond directly to measures in the NHSDA are lifetime prevalence of each drug (which directly reflects initiation), past-month prevalence of alcohol use, and past-month prevalence of cigarette use. Those measures constitute just 13 of the 37 numbers in Tables D.2, D.3, and D.4, and 5 of those 13 come from a single program (Project ALERT). Hence, we prefer combining, in some fashion, information concerning direct measures (the 13 just mentioned) with indirect measures (the other 24), even though that combination will inevitably be somewhat ad hoc.

2. As mentioned in Chapter Four, there is considerable variation in the magnitude of effects across programs, with a few showing very large reductions in use as measured by particular indicators and other programs showing reductions close to zero. There are at least three explanations for these differences. One is that some programs are simply better than others are. Another explanation is that programs that focus on a specific substance can sometimes

produce greater impacts on that substance alone than can a more general program that seeks to reduce all types of substance abuse.

3. There are differences in baseline use rates between treatment and control groups that exist despite baseline randomization into these groups. If the first explanation held, it might be appropriate to drop information from the programs that appear to have smaller effects, basing our effectiveness estimates on only a subset of the programs. We choose instead to weight information from all programs equally for several reasons: (1) Even programs that might be judged "weaker" based on Tables D.2, D.3, and D.4 have been declared to be exemplary model programs; (2) our goal is not to derive conclusions about how cost-effective some prevention programs are relative to others; (3) our approach provides a more conservative estimate of the effect of prevention overall; and (4) to the extent that prevention dollars are being spread equally across substance-specific and general model programs, weighting all programs equally seems like a sensible way of obtaining the average effect we can expect from expanding the funding of model prevention programs generally.

Table D.2

Prevention's Impact on Marijuana Use: Percentage Difference Between Program Recipients and Controls for Various Indicators at First Available Follow-Up Data Collection

	Project ALERT	Lifeskills	MPP	Project Northland
Lifetime prevalence	-4.9%	—	—	—
Annual use	—	—	—	-14.0%
Monthly use[a]	-5.8%	—	—	—
Monthly prevalence	-20.3%	-7.1%	-26.0%	—
Weekly use	-18.0%	-33.3%	-22.8%	—

[a]Project ALERT constructs a measure of regular monthly use of each substance from responses to the number of times within a year that the individual reported using the substance. If the response rates were greater than 12, then the respondent was considered to be a regular monthly user. This is different from the other programs, which reported estimates for past-month prevalence only ("Monthly prevalence" in this table).

Table D.3

Prevention's Impact on Tobacco Use: Percentage Difference Between Program Recipients and Controls for Various Indicators at First Available Follow-Up Data Collection

	Project ALERT	Project Northland	Project TNT[a]	Lifeskills	MPP
Lifetime prevalence	−4.3%	−19.2%	−21.5%	—	—
Monthly use	−0.7%	—	—	—	—
Monthly prevalence	−2.0%	—	—	−19.7%	−31.5%
Weekly use	−7.9%	—	−64.3%	−18.5%	−30.3%
Daily/pack a day	−1.6%	—	—	−20.8%	—

[a]Numbers shown for Project TNT represent the combined model intervention.

Table D.4

Prevention's Impact on Alcohol Use: Percentage Difference Between Program Recipients and Controls for Various Indicators at First Available Follow-Up Data Collection

	Project ALERT	Iowa	Lifeskills	MPP	Project Northland	Enhanced AMPS
Lifetime prevalence	−4.1%	−26.0%	—	—	—	—
Annual prevalence	—	—	—	—	—	−3.3%
Monthly use	−5.4%	—	—	—	—	—
Monthly prevalence	−2.1%	—	−1.7%	−30.8%	−19.2%	—
Weekly use	+2.2%	—	−8.6%	−42.0%	−29.1%	—
Heavy drinking	—	−24.4%	−16.3%	—	—	−4.5%

A related problem in developing an aggregate performance measure from these various program effects is the sparseness of the data. Fewer than half of the cells in Tables D.2, D.3, and D.4 are filled in. When comparing numbers in the tables, one is often comparing simultaneously across both programs and measures, which can make it difficult to untangle whether a large (or small) effect can be attributed to a particular program or is just specific to a particular indicator of use. For example, Project Northland reports effectiveness for only a single indicator of marijuana use (annual use) and tobacco use (lifetime prevalence). Furthermore, in the case of marijuana, Project Northland's estimate is the only one available for annual use. Compounding these problems is the issue of variability. The numbers in Tables D.2, D.3, and D.4 are point estimates. Particularly for indicators of heavy use, they are based on a relatively modest number of respondents and so are surrounded by moderately broad confidence intervals (which are not shown).

FOUR METHODS FOR COLLAPSING THE TABLE DATA INTO AGGREGATE PERFORMANCE MEASURES

Taken together, these complications imply that characterizing the performance of the typical model school-based prevention program involves considerable judgment, not mechanical mathematics. With that in mind, we focus on four methods for collapsing the information in Tables D.2, D.3, and D.4 into aggregate performance measures. The results from these methods are used to establish a range of possible values within which we suspect the true aggregate measure of program effectiveness will fall. (For symmetry's sake and because the values might be useful, we derive aggregate measures for lifetime and past-month prevalence for all three drugs—six measures in all—instead of just the three we use as predictors.)

Method 1: Direct Measures of Use

Our first approach is to use only measures of program effectiveness that correspond directly to variables in the NHSDA. The main advantage of this approach is that it maps specific research findings from the literature to their inferred effect for the general population as reflected by data from the NHSDA. The primary disadvantage is that we end up throwing out a lot of information on program effectiveness reflected in the other measures provided in these tables.

We calculate a composite measure of effectiveness for each measure of use by taking the average of the program effects reported by measure of use (see Table D.5). In the case of marijuana, only Project ALERT provides a direct measure of the intervention on marijuana initiation. Two programs provide direct measures of the intervention

Table D.5

Method 1: Average Program Effects by Measure of Use Using Direct Measures of Use

Substance	Measure of Use	Average Effect
Marijuana	Lifetime prevalence	–4.9%
	Past-month prevalence	–17.8%
Alcohol	Lifetime prevalence	–15.1%
	Past-month prevalence	–13.5%
Tobacco	Lifetime prevalence	–15.0%
	Past-month prevalence	–17.7%

on alcohol initiation (Project ALERT and Iowa Strengthening Families), and four provide direct measures of the effect on monthly prevalence (Project ALERT, Lifeskills, MPP, and Project Northland). For cigarettes, three programs provide direct estimates of effects on cigarette initiation (Project ALERT, Project Northland, and Project TNT) and three provide direct estimates of the intervention on past-month prevalence (Project ALERT, Lifeskills, and MPP). The far-right column of Table D.5 reports the simple averages obtained from those programs by measure of use.

Method 2: Assuming Prevention Affects All Measures of Use by Equal Proportions

Given that there is so little information available about the effectiveness of universal model programs, we would prefer to use all the findings reported in Tables D.2, D.3, and D.4. Even though the remaining measures reported in those tables do not correspond directly to measures in the NHSDA, they do provide some information about changes in use. Their inclusion would also help reduce the influence of large and/or small extreme values (e.g., the Iowa Strengthening Families findings).

The issue of how to best use this additional information depends on one's willingness to make particular assumptions regarding the information contained in these additional data. If we were to assume that prevention programs affect all indicators of use by equal proportions, then we could simply average across all measures of use for each drug, yielding the results presented in Table D.6. The marijuana

Table D.6

Method 2: Average Program Effects by Measure of Use Using Assumption of Proportionality

Substance	Measure of Use	Average Effect
Marijuana	Lifetime prevalence	−16.9%
	Past-month prevalence	−16.9%
Alcohol	Lifetime prevalence	−14.4%
	Past-month prevalence	−14.4%
Tobacco	Lifetime prevalence	−18.6%
	Past-month prevalence	−18.6%

averages, for example, are the average of all the numbers in Table D.2.[2]

A question that arises with this approach is whether such an assumption is realistic. Given that many prevention programs specifically target heavy use (e.g., Enhanced AMPS, Project Northland), it may be that program effects are greater on measures of heavier use than on measures of light or moderate use. Indeed, there is some evidence in Tables D.2, D.3, and D.4 to support that statement. We therefore propose an alternative way to incorporate these indirect measures of use.

Method 3: Pairing Direct Measures with Similar Indirect Measures

Given the possibility that program effects may be different in percentage terms on measures of heavier use than on measures of light use, we now take an approach that falls somewhere between the preceding two approaches. We supplement the values for each direct measure with those of a measure related in intensity of use. The values for annual prevalence are averaged in with those for lifetime prevalence, and the values for monthly use are averaged in with those for past-month prevalence.

When we compute these averages for each measure (see Table D.7), we see that for marijuana the program effect on past-month preva-

---

[2] By definition, if we assume that prevention affects all measures of use equally, the estimated impacts on past-month and lifetime prevalence are the same.

Table D.7

Method 3: Average Program Effects by Measure of Use Using the Weighted Average of All Measures

Substance	Measure of Use	Average Effect
Marijuana	Lifetime prevalence	–9.5%
	Past-month prevalence	–14.8%
Alcohol	Lifetime prevalence	–11.1%
	Past-month prevalence	–11.8%
Tobacco	Lifetime prevalence	–15.0%
	Past-month prevalence	–13.5%

lence is clearly greater than on lifetime prevalence. Alcohol shows a similar increasing average program effect from the lighter-use lifetime (combined with annual) prevalence measure to the moderate monthly measures, but the difference in effect is substantially smaller than that for marijuana. This is likely due to the fact that past-month drinking, our primary measure of moderate use, is far more normative than past-month marijuana use and therefore is probably less indicative of increased alcohol involvement. In the case of tobacco, we see that average program effect declines as we go from light to moderate measures of use. This again is likely due to the inadequacy of measures of past-month use at capturing heavier involvement with smoking cigarettes. One interpretation of these numbers is that it would be appropriate to group light and moderate measures of use of alcohol and tobacco, but not marijuana, into a single category, but we retain the separation for all three so that our technique is consistent across all three substances.

Method 4: Interpolation

Our fourth approach is to fill in some of the missing values for our direct measures of use in Tables D.2, D.3, and D.4 by interpolation, using the fact that many programs report results for multiple measures of use. For example, we try to infer how MPP affects marijuana lifetime prevalence by observing Project ALERT's effect on marijuana lifetime prevalence (–4.9%) and noting that MPP had a somewhat larger effect on monthly prevalence and weekly use (–26.0% and –22.8%, respectively) than did Project ALERT (–20.3% and –18.0%). Assuming that monthly prevalence and weekly use are both measures of roughly comparable intensities of use and that effects are proportional, one might infer that MPP's effect on lifetime prevalence would be $-4.9\% \times ([26.0\% + 22.8\%] / [20.3\% + 18.0\%]) = -6.2\%$. We applied this logic to impute lifetime prevalence effects for Lifeskills and MPP for lifetime marijuana and tobacco use. Similarly, we used information on the relationship between lifetime and past-month prevalence of tobacco use from Project ALERT to estimate the impact on past-month use of tobacco for Project TNT and Project Northland.

Interpolating the alcohol lifetime prevalence effect is problematic because there are no adequate bridges between monthly and weekly use and lifetime prevalence. Project ALERT reports effects for various indicators, but the effects on monthly prevalence and weekly use—from which the bridge would be built—are not statistically different from zero. Putting them in the denominator of a bridging calculation amplifies the effects of the variability, which is problematic. So we report no interpolated estimate for effects on lifetime prevalence of alcohol use.

For past-month use of alcohol, we use Project ALERT data to build a bridge for the Iowa Strengthening Families program, relying on the relationship between lifetime prevalence and past-month use. Therefore, we interpolate past-month use of alcohol for Iowa Strengthening Families as $-2.1\% \times (-26.0\% / -4.1\%) = -13.3\%$. In a similar fashion, we can use information on the relationship between monthly prevalence and heavy drinking from the Lifeskills program to interpolate an estimate of past-month use for the Enhanced AMPS program $(-1.7\% \times [-4.5\% / -16.3\%] = -0.5\%)$.

Using the actual and interpolated values for lifetime and past-month prevalence alone, we calculate the average program effects. The results are presented in Table D.8.

COMPOSITE RESULTS

All the averages are listed together in Table D.9. Perhaps the most striking feature of this table is that, with the exception of the lifetime marijuana prevalence results, the variation in estimates obtained from each of our four methods is modest, despite the significantly different assumptions underlying each. It is fortunate the results are

Table D.8

Method 4: Average Program Effects by Interpolation of Missing Values

Substance	Measure of Use	Average Effect
Marijuana	Lifetime prevalence	-5.4%
	Past-month prevalence	NA
Alcohol	Lifetime prevalence	NA
	Past-month prevalence	-11.3%
Tobacco	Lifetime prevalence	-17.7%
	Past-month prevalence	-14.4%

NOTE: NA = No additional information could be obtained by interpolating values.

Table D.9

Program Estimates from Four Different Approaches to Computing Average Program Effectiveness

Substance	Measure of Use	Method 1 Average Effect	Method 2 Average Effect	Method 3 Average Effect	Method 4 Average Effect
Marijuana	Lifetime prevalence	-4.9%	-16.9%	-9.5%	-5.4%
	Past-month prevalence	-17.8%	-16.9%	-14.8%	NA
Alcohol	Lifetime prevalence	-15.1%	-14.4%	-11.1%	NA
	Past-month prevalence	-13.5%	-14.4%	-11.8%	-11.3%
Tobacco	Lifetime prevalence	-15.0%	-18.6%	-15.0%	-17.7%
	Past-month prevalence	-17.7%	-18.6%	-13.5%	-14.4%

NOTE: NA = No additional information could be obtained by interpolating values.

as robust as they are with respect to the necessarily somewhat ad hoc assumptions made in the aggregation process.

The largest variation in estimates is in the estimates obtained for lifetime prevalence of marijuana. This is perhaps not surprising in light of the fact that we have the fewest measures of program effectiveness in the case of marijuana, and only one program (Project ALERT) provides information on our direct measure of use. We also remind readers that the lifetime prevalence number reported in

Table D.1 for Project ALERT is a composite point estimate of program effectiveness across three different types of baseline users and two different treatment groups (see the first section of this appendix). There is statistical error associated with its construction that is unique to this program, although all of the programs for which we provide estimates have sampling error.

We still need to infer one set of low, best-guess, and high estimates of Factor 4 for each substance. For the midpoint best guess, we simply take the midpoint of the range of numbers (the average of the minimum and maximum) shown in each row of Table D.9. For the low and high estimates, we take, in the case of lifetime prevalence, the minimum and maximum numbers for lifetime or annual prevalence reported in Tables D.2, D.3, and D.4. In the case of past-month prevalence, we have a greater number of data from which to draw and thus can afford to eliminate some outliers that appear either too low or too high to be credible. We thus take as the low and high estimates the second-lowest and second-highest of the numbers reported for any of the moderate-use or light-use indicators in Tables D.2, D.3, and D.4. The results are shown in Table D.10. Our principal interest is in lifetime prevalence for marijuana and tobacco and past-month prevalence for alcohol; the numbers in those particular rows in Table D.10 also appear in Table 4.5.

Table D.10

Final Estimates of Program Effectiveness on Predictive Measures

Substance	Measure of Use	Low Estimate	Middle Estimate	High Estimate
Marijuana	Lifetime prevalence	−4.9%	−10.9%	−14.0%
	Past-month prevalence	−7.1%	−16.3%	−26.0%
Alcohol	Lifetime prevalence	−3.3%	−13.1%	−6.0%
	Past-month prevalence	−1.7%	−12.8%	−30.8%
Tobacco	Lifetime prevalence	−4.3%	−16.8%	−21.5%
	Past-month prevalence	−1.6%	−16.1%	−31.5%

We present here the details of our estimation of short-term program effectiveness decay, which is summarized in Chapter Five. The methodology differed somewhat depending on the substance. To briefly summarize, we fit two curves for each of the three drugs for which we estimate short-term effects. For marijuana and alcohol, we fit both a linear and a quadratic curve. In the case of marijuana, the quadratic curve implies rapid initial decay followed by slower decay in later grades, and in the case of alcohol, it implies first slow then fast decay. For alcohol, we actually fit two pairs of curves, one pair for initiation without parental permission and one for any initiation (here, we use lifetime prevalence data because data on decay of the monthly use effect are not available). For tobacco, we fit two decay curves, one based on all available data and one based on a subset of those data that are of the highest quality.

PROGRAM EFFECTIVENESS DECAY FOR MARIJUANA

As Table 4.2 in Chapter Four showed, there was approximately a 5 percent difference in lifetime marijuana use between treatment and control groups at the end of the Project ALERT program, with the treatment group reporting the lower prevalence rate. From published data, we know that approximately 60 percent of this difference in treatment and control prevalence rates remained one year following the end of the program (ninth grade) and that by the senior year of high school (four years after the end of the program) the difference no longer remained. This means that we have to interpolate how fast program effectiveness decayed during two intermediate years (tenth and eleventh grade).

At least two hypotheses regarding the rate of decay during these two intermediate years are possible. First, program effectiveness might have decayed at a constant rate after the initial decay between eighth and ninth grades. This would imply a linear decay function between grades 9 and 12. Spreading the 60 percent uniformly over these three years, this implies reductions of 20 percentage points per year, with steps at 60 percent, 40 percent, 20 percent, and finally 0 percent. Alternatively, it might have been the case that decay occurred more quickly in the first years following the program than in later years. Certainly this happened for the very first year (when effectiveness decayed from 100 percent to 60 percent, or by 0.4) relative to the following three years on average (when effectiveness decayed by an average of 0.2 per year). This suggests a convex decay function. One way to fill in such a convex decay function is to fit a quadratic through the three points: 100 percent effect in the eighth grade, the observed 60 percent effect in the ninth grade, and no effect in the twelfth grade.

We graph in Figure E.1 the decay functions implied by each of these hypotheses. The difference in implied program effects for years 2 and 3 are not substantial, particularly if one keeps in mind that the initial difference at the end of the program was only 5 percent (scaled in the graph to equal 100 percent for purposes of exposition). Thus, in either case, the remaining program effectiveness in years 2 and 3 is not any greater than 2 percent and 1 percent, respectively.

PROGRAM EFFECTIVENESS DECAY FOR ALCOHOL

Although follow-up program data exist for alcohol from the Project ALERT study, the study reports that there were no significant differences in treatment and control prevalence rates for any of the alcohol measures. Small differences in treatment and control groups over time, therefore, amount to nothing more than noise. Hence, we rely solely on the information from the Iowa Strengthening Families study. Unfortunately, the Iowa Strengthening Families study supplied follow-up data for only one year post-program and for three measures (lifetime prevalence of any use, of use without permission, and of drunkenness among users). For two of the three measures,

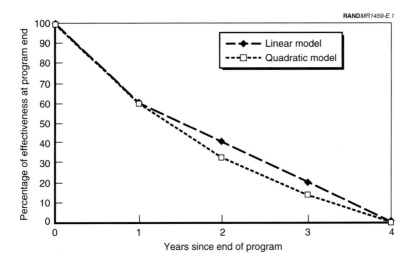

Figure E.1—Two Models of Decay of Effectiveness Against Marijuana Initiation

lifetime use for the full sample and drunkenness, the difference between treatment and control groups got larger, not smaller, suggesting "negative decay." This finding was consistent with findings in the ALERT data, although those differences in the ALERT data were not statistically different from zero.

We still assume that program effects dissipate by the twelfth grade for two reasons. First, we know that in a number of programs, such as TAPP, and not just in Project ALERT, all effects on alcohol use had disappeared by that grade even though we do not have data on how quickly those effects dissipated. Second, this assumption is consistent with what we know about program effects on tobacco and marijuana.

We focus on the lifetime prevalence measures (use with and without permission) because they are based on a larger sample, are consistent with the preceding analysis for marijuana, and are most relevant for our overall cost-effectiveness analysis agenda. Figure E.2 provides the resulting assumed decay trajectories with both a linear and a

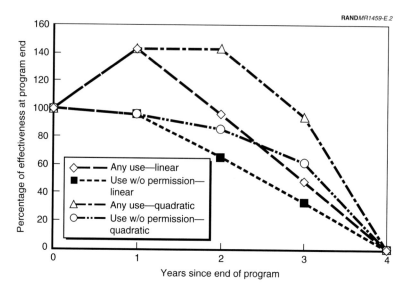

Figure E.2—Four Models of Decay of Effectiveness Against Alcohol Use

quadratic fit. Note that the difference between the models is larger than that for marijuana.

PROGRAM EFFECTIVENESS DECAY FOR TOBACCO

The richest data concerning how prevention program effects on any substance decay (or grow) as time elapses come from the Minnesota Smoking Prevention Program. Unfortunately, those data have a number of limitations, as a description of the evaluation makes clear.

The Minnesota Smoking Prevention Program consisted of two back-to-back studies of four treatment interventions (one "standard" intervention and three variants on an "innovative" intervention). In the first study, classes within two schools were randomly assigned to one of the four treatments. Project staff administered the program to seventh-grade students. In the second study, initiated the following year, the same design was used for new seventh-graders in the original two schools, and two new schools were added as a nonequivalent comparison group. In addition, regular classroom teachers who were trained by project staff administered the program. Follow-up surveys were administered six months after program end and then at the end of each of six successive years (five successive years for Study 2) except one, and results from these surveys were regularly published (Murray et al., 1984, 1987, 1988, 1989). This program, therefore, provides us with the most data on post-program effects with which to evaluate decay.

However, there are a few aspects of the Minnesota Smoking Prevention Program design and implementation that make these data inherently different from data on our model programs. First, a true control group is not included in either of the Minnesota studies and although a nonequivalent control group was added to the second study, data for this group were not collected for one year for which we have treatment group data (in addition to the year for which we have no treatment group data). Second, the rates of cigarette use for the various treatment groups at the start of the program were never published, so we do not have baseline numbers to control for initial differences in treatment groups or their nonequivalent control group (except for baseline nonusers). Third, at the six-month follow-up for both studies and one-year follow-up for the first study, the only data available pertain to average number of cigarettes used per week, and they are reported on a different scale than are levels of cigarette use at other points in time. Subsequent published studies show findings for other measures of cigarette use, including lifetime prevalence, weekly smoking, and daily smoking. Because we have no information on these other measures around the program's end, we have no way of knowing where to anchor the decay function for these measures.

The basic method we pursue is to posit a model of how prevention effects vary over time and then fit the model to the data. The parameters that give the "best" fit in the sense of minimizing the sum of the squared differences between the predicted and observed results are then expressed in terms of a program effect decay curve.

We adopt two different attitudes, or approaches, with respect to the data and their limitations:

- Approach 1: We throw out the weaker data and fit a very simple model to the remaining relatively small number of observations.

- Approach 2: We include more data but enrich the model in ways that might absorb or counterbalance the weaknesses introduced. Neither approach is entirely satisfactory, but relative to the current almost complete vacuum of information, these estimates may represent some incremental contribution. Measures included in the two approaches are shown in Table E.1 and explained in the following two sections.

Approach 1: Focusing on the Best Data

Three subsets of the Minnesota Smoking Prevention Program data are particularly problematic and are discarded in this first approach:

1. Data from Study 1 are discarded because Study 1 had no control group.

2. Data from baseline users (called "experimenters" in the study) are discarded because we have no data on their baseline use with which to adjust for differences in that use across treatment groups.

3. Data on lifetime prevalence are discarded because they are available for only two time periods in which there were control data (specifically, baseline and the one-year follow-up). These two time periods provide an estimate of the original effect, but a subsequent follow-up prior to the end of high school is required to provide any basis for estimating the shape of the decay curve.

In addition, we make several simplifying assumptions:

1. We fit only a simple exponential model of program effect over time: $E(t) = E0 \times \exp(-kt)$ where $E(t)$ is the percentage reduction in an indicator of use observed t years after the intervention, E0 is the initial effectiveness (as a percentage reduction in the same indicator), and k is the rate parameter governing the rate of decay.

2. For any given time period and measure, we average the percentage reductions observed across the four interventions rather than estimating models separately for each one. For example, the one-year follow-up data concerning the number of cigarettes smoked per week (by those who smoked) were 2, 3, 2.2, 3.7, and 12.3 for the four interventions and the nonequivalent comparison group (NECG), respectively. We converted those numbers for the four

Table E.1
Measures Taken in the Minnesota Smoking Prevention Program and Used in Decay Estimation Approaches 1 and 2

Calendar Year	Study Year Study 1	Study Year Study 2	Study 1 Baseline Users Tx Groups	Study 1 Baseline Nonusers Tx Groups	Study 2 Baseline Users Tx Groups	Study 2 Baseline Users NECG	Study 2 Baseline Nonusers Tx Groups	Study 2 Baseline Nonusers NECG
A Mid	0.5	—	Cigarettes per week	Cigarettes per week	—	—	—	—
A End	1	—	Cigarettes per week	Cigarettes per week	—	—	—	—
B Mid	—	0.5	—	—	Cigarettes per week	Cigarettes per week	Cigarettes per week[a]	Cigarettes per week[a]
B End	2	1	All[b]	All[b]	All[b]	All[b]	All[c]	All[c]
C End	3	2	—	—	—	—	—	—
D End	4	3	All[b]	All[b]	All[b]	All[b]	All[c]	All[c]
E End	5	4	All[b]	All[b]	All[b]	All[b]	All[c]	All[c]
F End	6	5	All[b]	All[b]	All[b]	All[b]	All[c]	All[c]

[a]Used in Approach 1 only.
[b]Used in Approach 2 only.
[c]Used in both approaches.

NOTE: All = cigarettes per week, weekly smoking, and daily smoking; neither approach uses lifetime prevalence. Tx = treatment. NECG = Nonequivalent comparison groups.

interventions into percentage reductions relative to the NECG (83.7 percent, 75.6 percent, 82.1 percent, and 69.9 percent, respectively) and took the average of those four percentage reductions (77.8 percent) as the effectiveness at reducing cigarettes smoked per week one year after intervention.

3. In two of three fitting exercises we did, we ignored the definitional difference in the measure of cigarettes smoked per week between the six-month follow-up and other times. Specifically, the six-month measure covered all subjects, whereas at other times the measure pertains only to those who smoke. This was deemed acceptable since we are focusing on percentage reductions from the NECG number at each follow-up. The third fitting exercise dropped the six-month data and yielded similar results, suggesting that this last simplification is not of great consequence.

The resulting "data" to which the exponential decay models were fit are summarized in Table E.2, and the best-fitting model parameters are given in Table E.3.

The models' fit is mediocre (the mean average percentage errors are high), even when excluding daily smoking's year-5 data point (which is negative). However, the parameter estimates are robust with respect to which data one fits (compare k values across the rows in Table E.3). Taken together, the results in Table E.2 suggest that the best fits are obtained by assuming a very large effect (100 percent or close to that) initially with a quite rapid decay (k around 0.42).

Table E.2

Average Percentage Reduction in Smoking Measures, Intervention Groups Relative to NECG

Time (Years Since Intervention)	Cigarettes Smoked per Week	Weekly Smoking	Daily Smoking
0.5	67.2%	—	—
1	77.8%	46.4%	62.0%
4	10.0%	16.7%	24.8%
5	12.1%	10.4%	−2.6%

NOTE: Years not listed lacked NECG data (one year also lacked treatment group data).

Table E.3

Resulting Best-Fitting Models

Data Used	Number of Data Points Fit	E0 (Reduction at Time 0)[a]	k (Decay Rate Parameter)	Mean Average Percent Error[b]
Cigarettes smoked per week	4	95.7%	0.419	29.0%
All data in Table E.2	10	96.1%	0.425	20.7%
All except six-month follow-up	9	100%[a]	0.417	21.3%

[a]E0 was constrained to be no more than 100%.

[b]Excludes daily smoking year-5 data point, which is negative; modeled effect must be non-negative.

Approach 2: Using Almost All Data

A second approach is to not aggregate across interventions and to retain all of the data except those pertaining to lifetime prevalence and the early data on number of cigarettes smoked per week, for which the measure is applied to everyone instead of just to smokers as it is in later follow-ups. Specifically, those are the six-month follow-up data and Study 1's one-year follow-up. We drop them here because, in contrast with Approach 1, we fit the model to the data themselves, not just to percentage changes in those data, so the difference in measures is problematic.

We fit the data themselves because, in including data on baseline users and data from Study 1, we have no information on baseline differences across intervention groups. Hence, it is not possible to estimate the effect size as *(change observed in treatment group – change observed in no-equivalent control group) / (change observed in nonequivalent control group)* and to fit to those percentage reductions. Instead we fit directly to the outcome data using a model that explicitly estimates the (uncontrolled) baseline differences across groups. This adjustment is necessarily ad hoc as we have no way to validate the model. The model is as follows:

$Y_{ijkt} = M_j \times b_i \times C_{kt} \times (1 - E_i \times [1 - D_t])$, where

i indexes the group (1 through 8 for the intervention groups and 9 for the NECG), j indexes the measure (cigarettes smoked per week, prevalence of daily smoking, prevalence of weekly smoking),

k indexes baseline use (0 for baseline nonsmokers, 1 for baseline smokers),

t indexes the time period (t = 1, 2, 3, 4, 5, 6, corresponding to years since implementation),

Y_{ijkt} = level of use observed in group i on measure j at time t among those with baseline level of use k,

M_j = level of measure j relative to that of reference measure,

b_i = adjustment for uncontrolled differences across groups relative to the NECG (so $b_9 = 1$),

C_{kt} = level of use at time t for a hypothetical control group with baseline use status k,

E_i = effectiveness of intervention i, that is, the fraction by which Y is lower in a treatment group relative to the control, and

D_t = decay in effectiveness, that is, the fraction of E that is gone, at time t.

Intuitively, the model allows the tobacco use measures to evolve over time differently and in a completely unconstrained manner for baseline users and nonusers, but the effects of differences across groups, differences across measures, and the prevention program effects themselves all enter multiplicatively, i.e., as percentage reductions relative to a reference group, a measure, or other program. For example, the students in one treatment group may have been at generally higher or lower risk for tobacco use than students in another treatment group. They may have been at equal risk, but we cannot rule out the other possibilities because students were not randomly assigned to treatment groups. In the model we fit, however, group-specific differences in risk appear as a group-specific percentage difference in measured use from that in the NECG, all other things equal. For example, one treatment group might be estimated to experience a level of use that is 10 percent higher than that in the NECG by virtue of its baseline characteristics alone, holding all other variables (including intervention effectiveness) constant across groups. Likewise, daily smoking prevalence is modeled as a simple multiple of cigarettes smoked per week (chosen as the reference measure).

Finally, the initial program effect (C_{k0}) is modeled as varying across treatment groups but not across measures (in percentage terms), and the decay is modeled as varying arbitrarily over time but not across treatment groups or measures. For example, if decay in year 3 is estimated to be 60 percent, then the model predicts that 60 percent of the initial effect disappears after three years in all groups and for all measures of use.

We sought parameter values that minimized the sum of the squared error between the predicted and observed levels of use for all 210 observations (across all relevant combinations of intervention or control group, baseline use category, year, and measure). The results reported in Table E.4 pertain to the case in which $E_9 = 0$ (since the nonequivalent control group received no intervention) and $E_1 = E_5$, $E_2 = E_6$, $E_3 = E_7$, and $E_4 = E_8$ (since each of those pairs of groups received essentially the same intervention, albeit in different years because they are different birth cohorts). In that case, there were 32 parameters (eight b_i's, four independent E_i's, one C_{0t}, C_{1t}, and E_t for each of the six time periods, and two M_j's because one M_j is arbitrarily set to 1).

We tried a number of variants of this model, including some that substantially reduced the number of parameters, e.g., by omitting the b_i's and by forcing the E_i's to be the same for all interventions. In some of these cases, the resulting decay was not monotonic, and we looked at results both with and without side constraining that forced the decay factors to be monotonically increasing.

It would be misleading to suggest that these variants all gave decay trajectories that were as consistent as for the three variants examined in Approach 1. Yet, with rare exception, they suggested that the vast majority (90-plus percent) of prevention's effect had decayed by six years post-intervention. In most cases the decay curve was convex, with larger declines (in percentage-point terms) in the earlier years, although by no means were the declines always as smooth as a classic exponential decay. Qualitatively, the biggest difference across

Table E.4

Coefficients Obtained When Fitting the Cigarette Use Decay Model

Program	b's	E's	Time	C_t (nonsmokers)	C_t (smokers)	D_t	Measure	M_j	Sum of Squared Errors
1PS	1.22	0.73	1	5.37	15.48	0.56	Ever smoked	1	2,313.14
1PSV	1.36	0.65	2	8.10	26.88	0.34	Weekly smoking	1.045	—
1ASV	1.13	0.46	3	10.78	31.38	0.44	Daily smoking	0.909	—
1AH	1.00	0.47	4	11.94	33.41	0.73	Cigarettes per week	1	—
2PS	1.05	0.73	5	15.92	38.55	0.83		—	—
2PSV	1.19	0.65	6	14.53	34.17	1.00		—	—
2ASV	1.15	0.46	—	—	—	—		—	—
2AH	1.14	0.47	—	—	—	—		—	—
2NECG	1	0	—	—	—	—		—	—

runs was that some suggested a larger decay after one year than after two, whereas for other runs, the opposite was true.

An intuitively appealing way of looking at the modeled decay over time is to compare for each treatment group observation the level of use actually observed and what the fitted model predicts would have happened in the absence of any intervention. The difference between the two can be expressed as the percentage reduction in use the model would attribute to the program; that percentage reduction in use is plotted over time in Figure E.3. There is a clear tendency for the percentage reductions in use to decrease over time, at least from year 2 on. The average of all such reductions by time period is given in Table E.5, both in raw terms and normalized to make the reduction at year 1 (the first period for which we have a result) scaled to be unity (100 percent). The reason for scaling is to show the decay profile from the original effect, in parallel to Figures E.1 and E.2. We arbitrarily set the result for year 1 to unity because this method

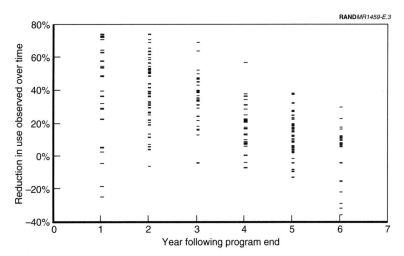

NOTE: Objects appearing to be rectangles are clusters of single tick marks.

Figure E.3—Observed Level of Cigarette Use as Percentage Reduction from Modeled No-Intervention Scenario, Full Distribution of Results, by Year Following Program End

Table E.5

Estimated Average Percentage Reduction in Level of Use Over Time

Year	Observed Level of Reduction in Use Relative to Modeled Counterfactual	Same Percentage Reduction Scaled to Be 100% at End of Year 1	Same Percentage Reduction Scaled to Be 100% at End of 8th Grade
1 (7th grade)	35.7%	100.0%	90.5%
2 (8th grade)	39.4%	110.0%	100.0%
3 (9th grade)	33.3%	93.0%	84.5%
4 (10th grade)	18.3%	51.1%	46.3%
5 (11th grade)	11.2%	31.4%	28.4%
6 (12th grade)	1.0%	2.9%	2.6%

provides us with no information as to what percentage of the end-of-program effect is left at the year-1 follow-up. That is, we do not know whether the 35.7 percent reduction observed in year 1 is half of an original reduction of 71.4 percent, indicating 50 percent decay in the first year, or is equal to a 35.7 percent end-of-program effect, indicating no decay in the first year, or any other possibility. Hence, all that these data really tell us about decay is what happens after year 1. In particular, what they suggest is that the programs have a bigger impact on smoking in year 2 than they do in year 1, and the effect in year 3 is nearly as great as it is in year 1, but it falls sharply between years 3 and 6 so that by year 6 very little of the effect observed as of year 1 remains.

These results pertain to measures of current smoking. Because we need a decay function for our predictor of lifetime cigarette use—that is, for lifetime prevalence—to calculate Factor 5 in the Table 2.1 model, we simply assumed that the decay function derived here for weekly and daily smoking also applies to lifetime prevalence. Table E.6 summarizes the decay curves. The alcohol figures are the simple average of the measures for lifetime prevalence of any use and of use without permission. For tobacco, we adopt for our model program, which we assume to take place in the eighth grade, the effectiveness in eighth grade as calculated from the decay models. Thus, for example, in Table E.5, we use the model shown in the right column, where the eighth-grade effect is taken to be 100 percent. We average across the Marijuana, Alcohol, and Tobacco columns in Table E.6 (with two fits for each of the three substances) to find an overall drug-independent model of decay.

In calculating "best guess" estimates for Table 2.2 in Chapter Two, we used the linear decay curve for all substances except cigarettes, for which we used Approach 2. These curves result in use reductions that fall between the other two measures (the second drug-specific measure and the drug-independent measure) relevant to each substance. In Appendix F, we will show that the curve one uses has only a modest impact on the final results, which is reassuring because the empirical evidence is so scant.

154 School-Based Drug Prevention: What Kind of Drug Use Does It Prevent?

Table E.6

Summary of Model of Decay in Effect Size (as Percent of Effect at End of Program in Grade 8)

Grade	Marijuana (Lifetime Prevalence)		Alcohol (Lifetime Prevalence)		Tobacco (Current Use)[a]		
	Linear	Quadratic	Linear	Quadratic	Approach 1	Approach 2	Average
8th	100	100	100	100	100	100	100
9th	60.1	60.1	119.2	119.2	65.7	84.5	84.8
10th	40.1	30.2	79.5	109.0	43.2	46.3	58.1
11th	20.0	10.2	39.7	69.3	28.4	28.4	32.7
12th	0	0	0	0	0	0	0

[a] Decay model used in estimating Factor 5. We assume the current-use decay model holds for lifetime tobacco prevalence.

EFFECTS ON LIFETIME CONSUMPTION

In this appendix, we elaborate on the results presented in Chapter Five. In that chapter, we reported a single effect on discounted lifetime consumption—the percentage reduction of cocaine use given the best-guess (mid-range) estimate of end-of-program effectiveness on the predictor variable, the optimistic scenario for the length of time deferred initiation was delayed, and the primary (linear) scenario for how short-term effectiveness decayed. That reduction-of-use number was 3.89 percent. In Chapter Five, we also provided values for Factor 5 (which is independent of short-term effectiveness) for all substances and delay scenarios but, again, for only the primary decay scenario. Here, we fill in the Chapter Five results completely, and add the alternate measure of problematic alcohol consumption—the frequency of having had at least five drinks at one sitting.

For any of the five lifetime substance-use-reduction measures (for four substances, including two measures for alcohol), we can show in a "three-dimensional" graph, such as Figure F.1, the results obtained by varying two of the three assumption sets. The figure illustrates the percentage reduction in lifetime cocaine consumption for each of the nine possible combinations of end-of-program effectiveness and initiation delay scenarios. Decay assumption—in this case, the general (drug-independent) decay curve—is held constant. The range in effects (1.9 percent to 9.7 percent) is similar to, but somewhat lower than, the range (2.9 percent to 13.6 percent) estimated by Caulkins et al. (1999). The difference stems primarily from our taking a more conservative approach to initiation delay. Specifically, the middle ("optimistic") scenario here corresponds to the most conservative scenario in the 1999 analysis.

Figure F.1 illustrates 9 of the 135 estimates (5 lifetime consumption-reduction outcomes, with 27 estimates per outcome—i.e., *three delay scenarios* times *three possible end-of-program effectiveness measures* times *three decay alternatives*). Including 14 more such figures in this appendix would be overwhelming, so we adopted the trick of "standing" to the right of each figure and examining each segmented shaded bar from the side, resulting in Figures F.2 through F.6 (see also Table F.1). The height of the bottom portion of each bar in Figures F.2 through F.6 shows the effect on lifetime consumption with the "conservative" initiation delay scenario. The middle portion shows the increment associated with moving from a conservative to an "optimistic" delay scenario, and the top portion shows the increment associated with moving from a more optimistic to a "very optimistic" stance with regard to delay of initiation. Therefore, the percentage corresponding to the very optimistic scenario is the percentage shown at the top of the bar.

We restrict our discussion here to those aspects of the findings not already presented in Chapter Five. The results for the two different problem-drinking outcomes (the frequency of consuming five-plus

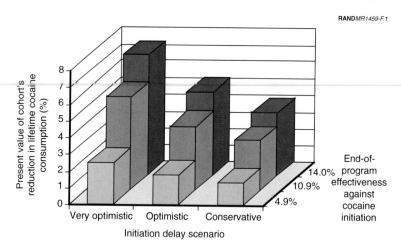

RAND*MR1459-F.1*

Figure F.1—Prevention's Estimated Effects on Lifetime Cocaine Consumption for Those Who Participate in a Prevention Program (with Drug-Independent Decay Curve)

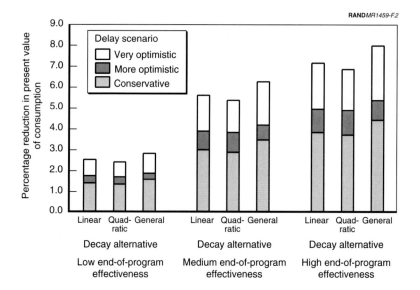

Figure F.2—Prevention's Effectiveness at Reducing Cohort's Lifetime Cocaine Consumption

drinks at a time and self-reported instances of drunkenness) are fairly similar. Effects with the conservative initiation delay scenario are a bit larger for drunkenness. However, the increment of projected effect when moving from a conservative to a more optimistic delay scenario is very small for self-reported instances of drunkenness (in contrast to the outcomes for five-plus drinks in one sitting). Thus, the effects with the optimistic and very optimistic scenarios are a little larger for the five-plus-drinks-at-a-time measure. But, in all other respects, the results are sufficiently similar that little is gained from trying to make distinctions between the two alcohol consumption measures.

Results other than those for alcohol are only modestly sensitive to the decay curve that is used. For marijuana and cocaine, results are largest with the general curve and smallest with the quadratic curve, which produce results up to 15 percent above and 5 percent below

Table F.1

Present Value of Prevention's Effectiveness at Reducing Lifetime Consumption (as a Percentage of Consumption Without Prevention)

Decay Alternative	Delay Scenario (Cocaine)			Delay Scenario (Marijuana)			Decay Alternative	Delay Scenario (Tobacco)		
	Conservative	Optimistic	Very Optimistic	Conservative	Optimistic	Very Optimistic		Conservative	Optimistic	Very Optimistic
Low End-of-Program Effectiveness										
Linear	1.35	1.75	2.51	0.78	1.73	2.40	Approach 1	0.53	0.96	1.80
Quadratic	1.28	1.71	2.41	0.77	1.66	2.28	Approach 2	0.60	1.01	1.90
General	1.55	1.88	2.80	0.92	1.95	2.77	General	0.62	1.03	1.96
Medium End-of-Program Effectiveness										
Linear	3.01	3.89	5.58	1.74	3.85	5.35	Approach 1	2.09	3.77	7.06
Quadratic	2.86	3.82	5.37	1.71	3.69	5.07	Approach 2	2.35	3.95	7.44
General	3.45	4.19	6.23	2.04	4.35	6.17	General	2.43	4.02	7.65
High End-of-Program Effectiveness										
Linear	3.86	4.99	7.16	2.24	4.94	6.87	Approach 1	2.67	4.81	9.02
Quadratic	3.67	4.90	6.89	2.19	4.74	6.51	Approach 2	3.00	5.04	9.51
General	4.43	5.38	8.00	2.62	5.59	7.92	General	3.11	5.14	9.78

Table F.1—Continued

Decay Alternative	Delay Scenario			Delay Scenario		
	Conservative	Optimistic	Very Optimistic	Conservative	Optimistic	Very Optimistic
	Self-Reported Instances of Drunkenness			Times Consuming Five-Plus Drinks at One Sitting		
Low End-of-Program Effectiveness						
Linear	0.29	0.36	0.53	0.24	0.40	0.60
Quadratic	0.37	0.41	0.62	0.32	0.47	0.72
General	0.22	0.30	0.44	0.18	0.32	0.48
Medium End-of-Program Effectiveness						
Linear	2.22	2.71	4.03	1.82	3.02	4.52
Quadratic	2.79	3.06	4.70	2.45	3.55	5.42
General	1.69	2.23	3.29	1.33	2.41	3.61
High End-of-Program Effectiveness						
Linear	5.33	6.52	9.69	4.38	7.25	10.86
Quadratic	6.72	7.35	11.30	5.88	8.53	13.03
General	4.07	5.37	7.91	3.20	5.79	8.67

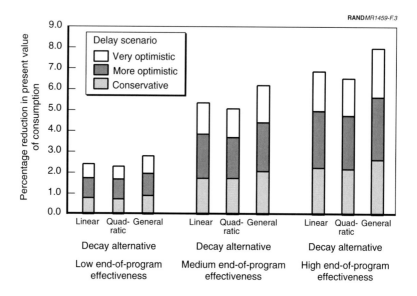

Figure F.3—Prevention's Effectiveness at Reducing Cohort's Lifetime Marijuana Consumption

those with the linear curve, respectively. For tobacco, the results are also largest for the general curve, but results with the two tobacco-specific approaches in Table E.6 in Appendix E are similar. Specifically, the results with Approach 2 are no more than 3 percent below the results with the general curve or 10 percent above the results with Approach 1. In contrast, the quadratic decay curve for alcohol produces estimated impacts that are almost half again as large as the impacts produced by the general decay curve.

Results are most sensitive to the assumptions about short-term effectiveness. In fact, the projections of impacts on lifetime use are proportional to the assumption about short-term effectiveness. So, the bars in Figure F.3 associated with a "high" marijuana prevention effectiveness of 14.0 percent are 2.9 times the height of those associated with a "low" marijuana prevention effectiveness of 4.9 percent (14.0/4.9 = 2.9). Dividing each bar by the short-term prevention effectiveness estimate converts these estimated impacts on lifetime use to estimated impacts on lifetime use per 1 percent reduction in

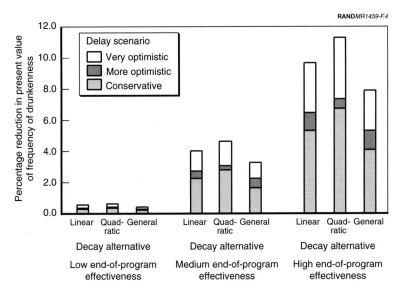

Figure F.4—Prevention's Effectiveness at Reducing Cohort's Lifetime Self-Reported Incidents of Drunkenness

use observed at the end of the prevention program (i.e., Factor 5). These percentage reductions in lifetime use per percentage reduction in use at the end of the program are all displayed in a single graph (see Figure F.7) to facilitate comparisons across substances.

As discussed in Chapter Five, the differences across drugs, as reflected in Figure F.7, stem from differences in expected lifetime consumption conditioned on age of initiation. For example, moving from a conservative to an optimistic permanence assumption effectively shifts some marijuana initiation from ages 16 to 18 to ages 19 to 21. Self-reported lifetime cocaine use is only modestly lower for those who initiate marijuana at ages 19 to 21 versus those who initiate at ages 16 to 18. (The big difference is between lifetime reported cocaine use for those who initiate marijuana before age 15 versus those who initiate after age 15.) In contrast, lifetime marijuana use is much lower for those initiating marijuana use at ages 19 to 21 than for those initiating marijuana at ages 16 to 18.

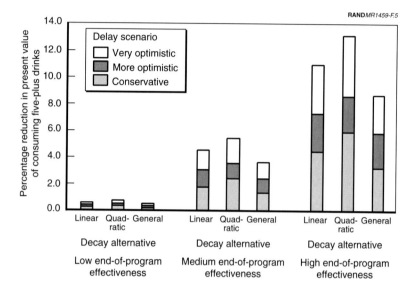

**Figure F.5—Prevention's Effectiveness at Reducing Cohort's Lifetime
Incidents of Consuming at Least Five Drinks at One Sitting**

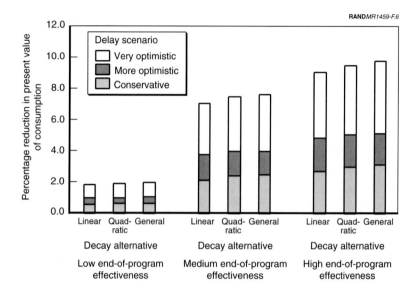

Figure F.6—Prevention's Effectiveness at Reducing Lifetime Cigarette
Consumption

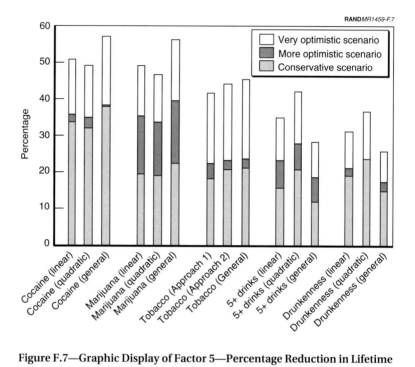

Figure F.7—Graphic Display of Factor 5—Percentage Reduction in Lifetime Use per Percentage Reduction in Use at End of Program, by Drug, Decay Curve, and Permanence Assumption

BIBLIOGRAPHY

Bachman, J. G., L. D. Johnston, and P. M. O'Malley "Explaining Recent Increases in Students' Marijuana Use: Impacts of Perceived Risks and Disapproval, 1976 and 1996," *American Journal of Public Health,* Vol. 88, No. 6, 1998, pp. 887–892.

Bartlett, J. C., L. S. Miller, D. P. Rice, and W. B. Max, "Medical Care Expenditures Attributable to Cigarette Smoking—United States 1994," *MMWR,* Vol. 43, 1994, pp. 469–472.

Becker G. S., *Human Capital,* New York: National Bureau of Economic Research, 1964.

Behrens, Doris A., Jonathan P. Caulkins, Gernot Tragler, and Gustav Feichtinger, "Optimal Control of Drug Epidemics: Prevent and Treat—But Not at the Same Time," *Management Science,* Vol. 46, No. 3, 2000, pp. 333–347.

Behrens, Doris A., Jonathan P. Caulkins, Gernot Tragler, and Gustav Feichtinger, "Why Present-Oriented Societies Undergo Cycles of Drug Epidemics," *Journal of Economic Dynamics and Control,* Vol. 26, No. 6, 2002, pp. 919–936.

Behrens, Doris A., Jonathan P. Caulkins, Gernot Tragler, Josef Haunschmied, and Gustav Feichtinger, "A Dynamic Model of Drug Initiation: Implications for Treatment and Drug Control," *Mathematical Biosciences,* Vol. 159, 1999, pp. 1–20.

Bernaards, Claire M., Jos W. R. Twisk, Jan Snel, Willem Van Mechelen, and Han C. G. Kemper, "Is Calculating Pack-Years Retrospectively a Valid Method to Estimate Life-Time Tobacco

Smoking? A Comparison Between Prospectively Calculated Pack-Years and Retrospectively Calculated Pack-Years," *Addiction*, Vol. 96, No. 11, 2001, pp. 1653–1661.

Botvin, Gilbert J., Eli Baker, Linda Dusenbury, Elizabeth N. Botvin, and Tracy Diaz, "Long-Term Follow-Up Results of a Randomized Drug Abuse Prevention Trial in a White Middle-Class Population," *Journal of the American Medical Association*, Vol. 273, No. 14, April 1995, pp. 1106–1112.

Boyum, David A., and Mark A. R. Kleiman, "Substance Abuse Policy from a Crime-Control Perspective," in James Q. Wilson and Joan Petersilia, eds., *Crime*, 2nd ed., San Francisco: ICS Press, 2001.

Brounstein, Paul J., and Janine M. Zweig, *Understanding Substance Abuse Prevention: Toward the 21st Century*, Washington, D.C.: Center for Substance Abuse Prevention, 1999.

Caulkins, Jonathan P., C. Peter Rydell, Susan S. Everingham, James Chiesa, and Shawn Bushway, *An Ounce of Prevention, a Pound of Uncertainty: The Cost-Effectiveness of School-Based Drug Prevention Programs*, Santa Monica, Calif.: RAND, MR-923-RWJ, 1999.

Centers for Disease Control, *Reducing Tobacco Use: A Report of the Surgeon General*, Executive Summary, U.S. Department of Health and Human Services, Centers for Disease Control and Prevention, National Center for Chronic Disease Prevention and Health Promotion, Office of Smoking and Health, Atlanta, Ga., 2000.

Chaloupka, F. J., and R. L. Pacula, "Economics and Anti-Health Behavior: The Economic Analysis of Substance Use and Abuse," in W. Bickel and R. Vuchinich, eds., *Reframing Health Behavior Change with Behavioral Economics*, Hillsdale, N.J.: Lawrence Erlbaum Associates, 2000, pp. 89–111.

Chaloupka, F. J., and K. E. Warner, "The Economics of Smoking," in J. Newhouse and A. Culyer, eds., *The Handbook of Health Economics*, Vol. 1B, Cambridge, Mass.: Harvard University Press, 2000.

Cohen, M. A., "Alcohol, Drugs and Crime: Is "Crime" Really One-Third of the Problem?" *Addiction*, Vol. 94, No. 5, 1999, pp. 644–647.

Cook, P. J., "The Social Costs of Drinking," in *Expert Meeting on Negative Social Consequences of Alcohol Use*, Oslo: Norwegian Ministry of Health and Social Affairs, 1991.

Cruze, A. M., H. J. Harwood, P. L. Kristiansen, J. J. Collins, and D. C. Jones, *Economic Costs to Society of Alcohol and Drug Abuse and Mental Illness—1977*, Research Triangle Park, N.C.: Research Triangle Institute, RTI/1925/00-14F, 1981.

Dozier, A. L., and M. J. Barnes, "Ethnicity, Drug User Status and Academic Performance," *Adolescence*, Vol. 32, No. 128, 1997, pp. 825–837.

Drug Strategies, *Safe Schools, Safe Students*, Washington, D.C.: Drug Strategies, 1994 and 1998.

Drug Strategies, *Making the Grade: A Guide to School Drug Prevention*, Washington, D.C.: Drug Strategies, 1995.

Ellickson, Phyllis L., "School-Based Substance Abuse Prevention: What Works, For Whom, and How?" in S. Kar, ed., *Substance Abuse Prevention: A Multicultural Perspective*, Amityville, N.Y.: Baywood Publishing Company, Inc., 1999.

Ellickson, P. L., R. M. Bell, and K. McGuigan, "Preventing Adolescent Drug Use: Long-Term Results of a Junior High Program," *American Journal of Public Health*, Vol. 83, No. 6, 1993, pp. 856–861.

Ellickson P. L., K. Bui, R. Bell, and K. A. McGuigan, "Does Early Drug Use Increase the Risk of Dropping Out of High School?" *Journal of Drug Issues*, Vol. 28, No. 2, 1998, pp. 357–380.

Elliott, Delbert S., ed., *Blueprints for Violence Prevention*, Boulder, Colo.: University of Colorado at Boulder, 1997.

Everingham, Susan S., and C. Peter Rydell, *Modeling the Demand for Cocaine*, Santa Monica, Calif.: RAND, MR-332-ONDCP/A/DPRC, 1994.

Flay, B. R., D. Koepke, S. J. Thomson, S. Santi, J. A. Best, and K. S. Brown, "Six-Year Follow-Up of the First Waterloo School Smoking

Prevention Trial," *American Journal of Public Health,* Vol. 79, 1989, pp. 1371–1376.

French, M. T., and G. A. Zarkin, "Is Moderate Alcohol Use Related to Wages: Evidence from Four Worksites," *Journal of Health Economics,* Vol. 14, 1995, 319–344.

Greenwood, Peter W., Karyn E. Model, C. Peter Rydell, and James Chiesa, *Diverting Children from a Life of Crime: Measuring Costs and Benefits,* Santa Monica, Calif.: RAND, MR-699-1-UCB/RC/IF, 1998.

Hall, W., and T. Babor, "Cannabis Use and Public Health: Assessing the Burden," *Addiction,* Vol. 95, No. 4, 2000, pp. 485–490.

Hall, W., L. Johnston, and N. Donnelly, "The Epidemiology of Cannabis Use and Its Consequences," in H. Kalant, W. Corrigall, W. Hall, and R. Smart, eds., *The Health Effects of Cannabis,* Toronto: Addiction Research Foundation, 1999, pp. 69–125.

Hanson, W. B., C. K. Malotte, and J. E. Fielding, "Evaluation of a Tobacco and Alcohol Abuse Prevention Curriculum for Adolescents," *Health Education Quarterly,* Vol. 14, No. 1, 1988, pp. 93–114.

Harwood, H., D. Fountain, and G. Livermore, *The Economic Costs of Alcohol and Drug Abuse in the United States 1992,* Bethesda, Md.: National Institute on Drug Abuse, NIH Publication 98-4327, 1998.

Harwood, H. J., D. M. Napolitano, P. L. Kristiansen, and J. J. Collins, *Economic Costs to Society of Alcohol and Drug Abuse and Mental Illness: 1980,* Research Triangle Park, N.C.: Research Triangle Institute, RTI/2734/00-01FR, 1984.

Hodgson, T. A., "Cigarette Smoking and Lifetime Medical Expenditures," *Milbank Quarterly,* Vol. 70, 1992, pp. 81–125.

Hoffman, John P., Cindy Larison, and Allen Sanderson, *An Analysis of Worker Drug Use and Workplace Policies and Program,* Rockville, Md.: Substance Abuse and Mental Health Services Administration, 1997.

Johnson, Robert A., Dean R. Gerstein, Rashna Ghadialy, Wai Choy, and Joseph Gfroerer, *Trends in the Incidence of Drug Use in the United States, 1919–1992*, Washington, D.C.: U.S. Department of Health and Human Services, Substance Abuse and Mental Health Services Administration, 1996.

Kandel, Denise, "Stages in Adolescent Involvement in Drug Use," *Science,* Vol. 190, 1975, pp. 912–914.

Kandel, D. B., and M. Davies, "Labor Force Experiences of a National Sample of Young Adult Men," *Youth and Society*, Vol. 21, No. 4, 1990, pp. 411–445.

Kandel, Denise, and Kazuo Yamaguchi, "From Beer to Crack: Developmental Patterns of Drug Involvement," *American Journal of Public Health,* Vol. 83, No. 6, 1993, pp. 851–855.

Keeler, Emmett B., and Shan Cretin, *Discounting of Nonmonetary Effects,* Santa Monica, Calif.: RAND, N-1875-HHS, 1982.

Kenkel, D. S., and P. Wang, "Are Alcoholics in Bad Jobs?" National Bureau of Economic Research Working Paper No. 6401, Cambridge, Mass., 1998.

Kleiman, Mark A. R., *Against Excess: Drug Policy for Results,* New York: Basic Books, 1992.

Kleiman, Mark A. R., "Enforcement Swamping: A Positive-Feedback Mechanism in Rates of Illicit Activity," *Mathematical and Computer Modeling*, Vol. 17, 1993, pp. 65–75.

Kott, Alan, and William Nottingham, *OASAS Evaluation Systems Behaviors of Clients Remaining in Treatment at Least Six Months,* New York State Office of Alcoholism & Substance Abuse Services, Albany, N.Y., September 1999. Available at http://www.oasas.state.ny.us/pio/research/eval0999.htm.

Maguire, Kathleen, and Ann L. Pastore, eds., *Sourcebook on Criminal Justice Statistics 1999,* U.S. Department of Justice, Bureau of Justice Statistics, Washington, D.C.: U.S. Government Printing Office, 2000.

Marston, A. R., D. F. Jacobs, R. D. Singer, M. F. Widaman, and T. D. Little, "Adolescents Who Apparently Are Invulnerable to Drug, Alcohol, and Nicotine Use," *Adolescence*, Vol. 23, No. 91, 1998, pp. 593–598.

Mensch, B. S., and D. B. Kandel, "Dropping Out of High School and Drug Involvement," *Sociology of Education*, Vol. 61, 1988, pp. 95–113.

Miller, L. S., X. Zhang, D. P. Rice, and W. Max, "State Estimates of Total Medical Expenditures Attributable to Cigarette Smoking, 1993," *Public Health Report*, Vol. 113, 1999, pp. 447–458.

Mincer, J., "The Distribution of Labor Incomes: A Survey with Special Reference to the Human Capital Approach," *Journal of Economic Literature*, Vol. 8, No. 1, 1970, pp. 1–26.

Model, K. E., "The Effect of Marijuana Decriminalization on Hospital Emergency Room Drug Episodes: 1975–1978," *Journal of the American Statistical Association*, Vol. 88, No. 423, 1993, pp. 737–747.

Mullahy, J., and J. L. Sindelar, "Alcoholism, Work, and Income," *Journal of Labor Economics*, Vol. 11, 1993, pp. 494–520.

Murray D., M. Davis-Hearn, A. I. Goldman, P. Pirie, and R. V. Luepker, "Four- and Five-Year Follow-up Results from Four Seventh-Grade Smoking Prevention Strategies," *Journal of Behavioral Medicine*, Vol. 11, No. 4, 1988, pp. 395–405.

Murray, D., R. V. Luepker, C. A. Johnson, and M. B. Mittlemarke, "The Prevention of Cigarette Smoking in Children: A Comparison of Four Strategies," *Journal of Applied Social Psychology*, Vol. 14, No. 3, 1984, pp. 274–288.

Murray, D., P. Pirie, R. V. Luepker, and U. Pallonen, "Five- and Six-Year Follow-Up Results from Four Seventh-Grade Smoking Prevention Strategies," *Journal of Behavioral Medicine*, Vol. 12, No. 2, 1989, pp. 207–218.

Murray, D., P. S. Richards, R. V. Luepker, and C. A. Johnson, "The Prevention of Cigarette Smoking in Children: Two- and Three-

Year Follow-Up Comparisons of Four Prevention Strategies," *Journal of Behavioral Medicine*, Vol. 10, No. 6, 1987, pp. 595–611.

Musto, David F., *The American Disease: Origins of Narcotic Control*, New York: Oxford University Press, 1987.

National Institute on Alcohol Abuse and Alcoholism, *see NIAAA*.

National Institute on Drug Abuse (NIDA), *Some Research-Based Drug Abuse Prevention Programs*, Bethesda, Md., 1999.

NIAAA, "Volume Beverage and Ethanol Consumption for States, Census Regions, and the United States, 1970–98," 2001a. Available at http://www.niaaa.nih.gov/databases/consum02.txt.

NIAAA, "Apparent per Capita Ethanol Consumption for the United States, 1850–1998," 2001b. Available at http://www.niaaa.nih.gov/databases/consum01.txt.

Office of National Drug Control Policy (ONDCP), Office of Programs, Budget, Research, and Evaluations, *What America's Users Spend on Illegal Drugs 1988–1998*, Washington, D.C., 2000.

Pentz, Mary Ann, "Cost, Benefits, and Cost-Effectiveness of Comprehensive Drug Abuse Prevention," in *Cost-Benefit/Cost-Effectiveness Research of Drug Abuse Prevention: Implications for Programming and Policy*, Washington, D.C.: U.S. Department of Health and Human Services, NIDA Research Monograph 176, 1998, pp. 111–129.

Pentz, M. A., J. H. Dwyer, D. P. MacKinnon, B. R. Flay, W. B. Hansen, E. Y. Wang, and C. A. Johnson, "A Multi-Community Trial for Primary Prevention of Adolescent Drug Abuse: Effects on Drug Use Prevalence," *Journal of the American Medical Association*, Vol. 261, 1989, pp. 3259–3266.

Peterson, A. V., K.I.A. Kealey, S. L. Mann, P. M. Marek, and I. G. Sarason, "Hutchinson Smoking Prevention Project: Long-Term Randomized Trial in School-Based Tobacco Use Prevention—Results on Smoking," *Journal of the National Cancer Institute*, Vol. 92, No. 24, 2000, pp. 1979–1991.

Polen, M., S. Sidney, I. S. Tekawa, M. Sadler, and G. D. Friedman, "Health Care Use by Frequent Marijuana Smokers Who Do Not Smoke Tobacco," *Western Journal of Medicine,* Vol. 158, 1993, pp. 596–601.

Register, C., and D. Williams, "Labor Market Effects of Marijuana and Cocaine Use Among Young Men," *Industrial and Labor Relations Review,* Vol. 45, No. 3, 1992, pp. 435–448.

Reuter, Peter, and Mark Kleiman, "Risks and Prices: An Economic Analysis of Drug Enforcement," in Norval Morris and Michael Tonry, eds., *Crime and Justice: A Review of Research,* Chicago: The University of Chicago Press, 1986, pp. 289–340.

Reuter, Peter, and P. Michael Timpane, *Options for Restructuring the Safe and Drug-Free Schools and Communities Act,* Santa Monica, Calif.: RAND, MR-1328-EDU, 2001.

Rice, D. P., T. A. Hodgson, P. Sinsheimer, W. Browner, and A. N. Kopstein, "The Economic Costs of the Health Effects of Smoking," *Milbank Quarterly 1986,* Vol. 64, No. 4, 1984, pp. 489–547.

Rice, D., S. Kelman, L. S. Miller, and S. Dunmeyer, *The Economic Costs of Alcohol and Drug Abuse and Mental Illness: 1985,* San Francisco: Institute for Health & Aging, University of California, 1990.

Robson, L., and E. Single, *Literature Review of Studies on the Economic Costs of Substance Abuse,* Canadian Centre on Substance Abuse, Toronto, March 1995. Available at http://www.ccsa.ca/costs/costslit.htm.

Rydell, C. Peter, and Susan S. Everingham, *Controlling Cocaine: Supply Versus Demand Programs,* Santa Monica, Calif.: RAND, MR-331-ONDCP/A/DPRC, 1994.

SAMHSA, *Preliminary Results from the 1995 National Household Survey on Drug Abuse,* Rockville, Md., 1996a.

SAMHSA, Office of Applied Studies, *National Household Survey on Drug Abuse Advance Report # 18,* Rockville, Md., 1996b.

SAMHSA, *Preliminary Results from the 1996 National Household Survey on Drug Abuse,* Rockville, Md., 1997.

SAMHSA, *Preliminary Results from the 1997 National Household Survey on Drug Abuse,* 1998.

SAMHSA, *Summary of Findings from the 1998 National Household Survey on Drug Abuse,* Rockville, Md., 1999a.

SAMHSA, Office of Applied Studies, *Year-End 1998 Emergency Department Data from the Drug Abuse Warning Network,* Rockville, Md., 1999b.

SAMHSA, *Drug Abuse Warning Network Annual Medical Examiner Data, 1999,* Washington, D.C.: U.S. Government Printing Office, 2000a.

SAMHSA, *Summary of Findings from the 1999 National Household Survey on Drug Abuse,* Rockville, Md., 2000b.

SAMHSA, Office of Applied Studies, *Treatment Episode Data Set (TEDS): 1993–1998,* Drug and Alcohol Services Information System Series: S-11, Rockville, Md., September 2000c.

SAMHSA, *Year-End 1999 Emergency Department Data from the Drug Abuse Warning Network,* Washington, D.C.: U.S. Government Printing Office, 2000d.

Shannon, D. M., F. R. James, and B. M. Gansneder, "The Identification of Adolescent Substance Misuse Using School-Reported Factors," *The High School Journal,* Dec/Jan 1993, pp. 118–128.

Shope, Jean T., Deborah N. Kloska, T. E. Dielman, and Ruth Maharg "Longitudinal Evaluation of an Enhanced Alcohol Misuse Prevention Study (AMPS) Curriculum for Grades Six–Eight," *Journal of School Health,* Vol. 64, No. 4, April 1994, pp. 160–166.

Society of Actuaries, *Transactions,* Vol. XXXIII, Schaumburg, Ill., 1982, pp. 343, 618. Actuarial life tables are downloadable through http://www.soa.org/tablemgr/tablemgr.asp.

Substance Abuse and Mental Health Services Administration, U.S. Department of Health and Human Services. *See SAMHSA.*

Sussman, S., C. W. Dent, A. W. Stacy, C. Hodgson, D. Burton, and B. R. Flay, "Project Towards No Tobacco Use: Implementation, Process and Posttest Knowledge Evaluation," *Health Education Research: Theory and Practice*, Vol. 8, 1993, pp. 109–123.

Thomas, C., *Marijuana Arrests and Incarceration in the United States: Preliminary Report*, research brief, Marijuana Policy Project, Washington, D.C., 1998. Available at http://www.mpp.org/arrests/prisoners.html.

Tobler, Nancy S., "Meta-Analysis of Adolescent Drug Prevention Programs: Results of the 1993 Meta-Analysis," in William J. Bukoski, ed., *Meta-Analysis of Drug Abuse Prevention Programs*, U.S. Department of Health and Human Services, NIDA Research Monograph 170, 1997, pp. 5–68.

Tonry, Michael, and James Q. Wilson, eds., *Drugs and Crime*, Chicago: The University of Chicago Press, 1990.

Warner, K. E., T. A. Hodgson, and C. E. Carroll, "Medical Costs of Smoking in the United States: Estimates, Their Validity, and Their Implications," *Tobacco Control*, Vol. 8, No. 3, 1999, pp. 290–300.

Yamada, T., M. Kendix, and T. Yamada, "The Impact of Alcohol Consumption and Marijuana Use on High School Graduation," *Health Economics*, Vol. 5, 1996, pp. 77–92.